Awakening Your Toddler's Love of Learning

BY JAN KATZEN-LUCHENTA

Karen,
Best to you +
your family
Jan

Emunah Publishing Company
Phoenix, Arizona

First Published in 1999 by
Emunah Publishing Company
PO Box 45148
Phoenix, Arizona 85064

Book design by The Write Advantage, Inc.
Scottsdale, Arizona

Printed by ONE CALL PRINTS ALL
Mesa, Arizona

Editorial Services by Erin Murphy
Flagstaff, Arizona

Illustrations by Carrie Follrad-Klein
Mesa, Arizona

ISBN 0-9665651-4-2

Contents

Preface vii

Acknowledgments...xi

Introduction: A Stroll Down the Road
        Less Toddled...xv

1 The Importance of Language and Communication

Words Are Your Toddler's Best Friends 3

Using Phonetic Sounds to Present Language 5

Language Presentation Exercises...........................11

Creating Activities That Advance Concentration,
        Verbal, and Fine Motor Skills 15

Enrichment and Expression of Vocabulary through
        Toddler-Appropriate Literature 23

Modeling Language to Support Your Toddler's
        Concentration Skills 26

2 Honoring Your Toddler's Physical and Emotional Boundaries

Tantrums No More 33

Four Steps to Resolving Emotional Conflict 35

    1. Acknowledge Feelings 35

    2. Put on Your Detective Hat.......................35

    3. Explain Why 36

    4. Give Choices That Lead to a Win-Win
        Resolution...36

Ten Ways to Avoid Emotional Conflict 41

    1. Resolve Conflicts Fairly...............................41

    2. Respect Your Child's Concentration 47

    3. Always Ask "May I?" 50

    4. Wipe and Blow Little Noses Gently 53

    5. Support Your Child's Bathroom
        Independence 56

    6. Inspire Peace at Mealtime 60

    7. Allow Your Child to Develop an Intimate
        Relationship with Nature.......................62

    8. Understand Your Child's Sense of Order 64

    9. Replace Convenient Objects Used to Comfort
        Your Child...67

       Alex's Story *72*

    10. Communicate through Your Eyes 75

3 Pausing to Look at Your Child

Developing a Teaching Relationship with
        Your Toddler 81
Healing and Preventing Attention and
        Speech Challenges 84
    Attention Challenges...............................84
        Jackie's Story *87*
        David's Story *88*
    Speech Challenges...............................95
        Andy's Story *97*
Designing a Home/School Environment That
        Supports Your Toddler 101
    Kitchen 102
    Living Room 106
    Bathroom 108
    Bedroom 109
    Outdoors..112
Toddler Needs and Tendencies 115
    Order 116
    Orientation 116
    Exploration...117
    Communication 117
    Activity 117
    Manipulation 118
    Work 118

Abstraction..119

Exactness 120

Repetition 120

Self-Perfection...121

4 125 Activities to Awaken Your Toddler's Love of Learning

How to Give an Activity Presentation
             to Your Toddler.....................................125

Activities of Practical Life (Basic Living Skills)......130

Activities to Refine the Senses 158

Activities for Language Development 163

Activities to Introduce Mathematics....................171

5 An Illustration of the Importance of Language and Communication

A Final Thought 175

Little Wind 175

Preface

A multitude of educators have dedicated their lives to the study of childhood. Maria Montessori, an Italian doctor who created an innovative methodology for teaching and understanding child development, has been my greatest inspiration. In all my years of teaching and utilizing her techniques, I've never seen a child who has not flourished in the classroom.

Except one . . . Nicky.

Nicky was twenty-six months old when he entered my classroom. I can remember how his sparkling blue eyes would light up with joy as he wandered around the classroom looking for an activity. Once he sat down with a project, he was committed to its completion. His sense of accomplishment and esteem felt so good to him that he became violent if anyone or anything posed a threat to his concentration. Sometimes he would even throw the activity he was working on at another child who was simply watching him.

Finally, Nicky split a little girl's forehead open with a block. Prompted by angry parents and the need to provide a safe environment for all of my students, I decided the best place for Nicky was out of the company of other children.

It was the only time in my teaching career that I made that decision. It wasn't easy because Nicky was doing so well. His periods of concentration had increased dramatically and he was beginning to express himself using audible language. Because of a deep-seated emotional wound, however, Nicky could not control his anger.

I spoke to his mother, and she told me that her sister-in-law would take care of Nicky. I felt a sense of relief and then sadness. How would Nicky's needs as a growing child be met? I offered to jot down a few notes for Nicky's new caregiver about how to set up an enriched environment at home. Those few notes turned into many pages and then into this book. That was two and a half years ago, and I'm still making notes.

In this book I have outlined ideas and suggestions for parents, extended families, preschool teachers, and anyone who wants to gain a simple understanding of how and when to relate to the toddler in a supportive, not destructive, manner.

Relating is such a small word for all it encompasses. It means respectful communication, timing, emotional tone and tempo of speech, eye contact, body language, love, example, consequence, consistency, and role modeling. And that's just relating to the toddler on a personal level.

Another aspect of relating to the toddler comes through the prepared environment—an environment at home or school in which the toddler can reach out and take from it anything he needs to expand and grow physically, cognitively, and spiritually.

If those modes of activity are not available for the toddler, he will become frustrated, sad, and stifled, just as flowers wilt and fail when their thirsty roots are not placed in fertile soil.

Special Note: *Girls and boys are equally precious to me, but for simplicity and readability, I use the pronoun "he" throughout this book.*

Acknowledgments

Many people, little and big, have made indelible imprints that have inspired and charted my course through toddler language interpretation. Without their distinct gifts, the pages of this book would be blank.

I dedicate this book to my mother, Dorothy. You have given me the greatest gift of all: life and the vicissitudes of sensitivity that enable me to experience it fully.

Special thank-yous to the following:

Nimal Vaz, my trainer and mentor—I'll always be grateful for your adherence to the Association Montessori Internationale's* education program. Without your pure preservation and exemplification of Dr. Montessori's concrete and theoretical teaching techniques, I could never embody her spirit and truly understand the word "disciple."

*Association Montessori Internationale (AMI) is a training course established by Dr. Maria Montessori in 1929. Its authenticity and reliable authority is internationally recognized, and is upheld by Dr. Montessori's family.

The Montessori Educational Center and the Reed Foundation, who provided scholarships that enabled me to take the AMI primary training.

Rhonda Baugh—I value your recommendation that I teach in the toddler classroom and your acceptance of my AMI internship.

Shirley Mars—I learned so much about positive communication and language development from your example.

Peg and Ed Huffman—I appreciate the beautiful, spacious classroom you provided for me so I could experiment, fumble, and victoriously realize the meaning of "the prepared environment."

Jodene Tryon—Your trust in my experience provided fertile soil in which my love, patience, and divine reverence for the child could blossom.

Robin Spaulding, for creating a space for me to continue "teaching" as I consult with families and caregivers pursuing a Montessori preschooling environment in their homes and schools.

Felicia Miller, for your gentleness, hard work and excellence in assisting me over the years.

Julie George, teaching assistant, friend, believer in my vision—Your devotion to Montessori education for toddlers of all socioeconomic and ethnic backgrounds is just one aspect of the size of your heart.

My greatest teachers have been the toddlers and their families who have shared the depths of their humanity with me over the years. I am beholden to you for teaching me the concrete meaning of the word that's been so abstract to me most of my life: love. You have shown me that respect, feelings, and relationships are the cornerstone of education and all of life.

A special acknowledgment goes to Mathew— Your emotional honesty brought me to a new consciousness; embracing you was more important than not getting mucus on my new silk blazer.

Brian Visel—It amazes me how you've turned indiscernible scribbles into this beautiful manuscript.

Book designer Vickie Mullins—I appreciate you transforming pages of outlines and text into this magical display of visual art.

Peggy Biniek, Laura Barnes, Georgette Cohen, Jessica Luchenta, Bob Davidson, and Mary Ellen Maunz, for helping me through the labyrinth of proofreading and editing.

Jessica, I need to acknowledge you again for your relentless pursuit of excellence and generosity of talent and time.

Senior editor Erin Murphy—Your experience and expertise in the publishing marketplace has proved to be an invaluable asset.

Time and experience have been special friends that have introduced me to Satwant and Jaswant Khalsa. They have given me the distinct opportunity to teach at the Khalsa Montessori School in Phoenix, Arizona. I share a beautiful toddler house with my wonderful assistant, Dolly, and ten "little ones" who come each day to find themselves.

My beloved husband, Joe, who continues to teach me the concrete meaning of the concept of love—Your presence in my life is like a symphony. Without it there would be no music.

Introduction: A Stroll Down the Road Less Toddled

Toddlers are an active, inquisitive lot—so much so that this age can be a difficult one for parents and toddlers both. Toddlers' communication and fine motor skills are limited, yet their strong desire for independence can frustrate the most devoted parents. From the parents' point of view, a toddler is "grown up" one minute and an infant the next.

How do we understand each other? Let's take a stroll down the road less toddled and see.

Just think what it would be like if suddenly your two-year-old could speak clearly within the context of "articulate assertive communication." What would be the ten most common requests your toddler might make of you?

1. Please don't grab things out of my hands or touch my activities without asking, "May I?" You'll be respecting my personal space and giving me a choice, and I'll probably say "yes."

2. Slow . . . down . . . your . . . speech. Crisply enunciate beginning, middle, and ending sounds in all words. You will make it easier for me to understand what you're saying and help me to communicate my thoughts and feelings earlier.

3. If I am in deep concentration, please wait until I take a break before you wipe my nose. Better yet, show me how to wipe my own nose (and always keep boxes of tissues on hand within *my* reach).

4. Please look into my eyes when I am talking to you or you are talking to me. Bend down if you must. If you wear glasses, take them off. This will in- crease my visibility into your eyes and heart. A fringe benefit is that you will have my undivided attention, which will promote good concentration skills throughout my life.

5. Talk lovingly to me even when I've made a mistake. Tenderness will attract my attention and compliance much quicker than yelling. Remember, your emotional energy is contagious.

6. Please don't say anything if I get food all over my face and in my lap as I feed myself. I'll clean it up if you show me how. I am perfecting a new skill. Nature didn't just graft wings together to make a

butterfly; allow me to be a gooey, messy caterpillar for a while.

7. I want and need to be with you and feel like I'm a contributing member of the household. Stop buying me toys that have no purpose. Set up tables, chairs and work areas in every room of the house that are my size. Let me sand wood with Dad or peel carrots with Mom. (If you're nervous about my cutting myself, you can dull any sharp peeler or knife with an emery board).

8. Please don't interrupt me when I'm talking or speak for me. I might become shy or stutter, and you'll have to drive me to the speech pathologist later on.

9. Always pay attention to my nutritional needs. Serve me foods that will give me an inner sense of peace and harmony. This might mean you'll have to get out of bed twenty minutes earlier to prepare a balanced breakfast. I'll gladly get up with you if you let me help and we eat breakfast together.

10. Make sure my living environment is designed for my complete sensorial exploration. I see with my fingers and sometimes even my mouth. Inhibiting that deep craving within me would be like having

someone put a blindfold over your eyes while you are trying to enjoy a beautiful sunset.

If we look into our own eyes, feelings, needs, and hearts, we gain a simple understanding of the toddler's seemingly unexplainable behavior and language, even when there are no words.

1 The Importance of Language and Communication

Words Are Your Toddler's Best Friends

Young children are thirsty to understand the sights, sounds, tastes, scents, and textures in their new world. For children of a certain age, mouthing or touching objects is the only way to satisfy this inquisitive sensory craving. Suddenly, what was viewed as black and white through the eyes of an infant or young toddler becomes a Surround Sound, Technicolor experience through mouthing or holding. That is why it is important that a child's environment be safe for complete sensorial exploration.

As adults, we have become so accustomed to sensory bombardment that silence attracts our attention more than the blasting audio of our television.

Everything feels new and exciting to the toddler: a telephone ringing, a dog barking, an air conditioner's mechanical hum. It's as if fireworks are going off all around the child. As adults, we have become so accustomed to sensory bombardment that silence attracts our attention more than the blasting audio of our television. We have already categorized most sensations into our subconscious; we understand their relationship to us. We cannot forget that the toddler yearns to gain the same understanding and insight into his world, yet physiologically might not be able to do so.

Research indicates that the brain's vast capabilities of transmitting, receiving, and retrieving messages form during the first three years of life. Because of the intricate nature of this phenomenon, it is important to realize that the memory of the small child functions differently than that of adults.

Consider this: An eighteen-month-old is startled and grabs onto his father's leg as he hears the loud, whirling sound of an ambulance siren. Dad comforts him, saying, "It's okay. That loud noise is coming from an ambulance. An ambulance is a van that helps people." The next time the child hears the loud siren of the ambulance, he still moves close to his dad in fear. Once again, his father lovingly reassures him. Repetition is the key until the child is capable of recollection and can identify the experience as one that is nonthreatening.

Something magical happens once the child can articulate (or attempt to articulate) the symbol or word for the experience himself. The word *ambulance* becomes a vehicle of affiliation and understanding. The fear of the overwhelmingly loud noise dissipates.

The child is learning to identify and categorize his world. He finds comfort and esteem in saying, "Ambulance—a van that helps people." For adults, it's like standing in a stadium full of people, feeling lost, then seeing the smiling eyes of a friend.

Words are your toddler's best friends. They are bridges of understanding and passages that seed all of humanity.

Using Phonetic Sounds to Present Language

Use objects whose beginning sounds are phonetic. This makes it easier for the child to recognize individual sounds (decode) and build words (encode), which prepares him for reading and writing. Start with words that contain one syllable, such as *hat, dog, lamp, cup, pen,* etc. Intermittently, present objects whose words each contain more than one syllable. This will keep the exercise challenging for the child who likes to repeat everything, though he may not be able to do so perfectly.

Phonetic Sound Examples:

a—apple   c—cat

b—book   d—dog

e—elephant

f—fan

g—gum

h—hat

I—itch

j—jar

k—kitten

l—lion

m—mother

n—nap

o—octopus

p—puppy

q—queen

r—rabbit

s—soap

t—tooth

u—umbrella

v—violin

w—water

x—x-ray

y—yellow

z—zipper

Make a list of words next to each beginning phonetic sound:

a _____   _____

    _____   _____

b _____   _____

    _____   _____

c _____   _____

    _____   _____

d _____   _____

_____   _____

e _____   _____

_____   _____

f _____   _____

_____   _____

g _____   _____

_____   _____

h _____   _____

_____   _____

i _____   _____

_____   _____

j _____   _____

_____   _____

k _____   _____

_____   _____

l _____   _____

_____   _____

m _____   _____

_____   _____

n _____   _____

_____   _____

o _____   _____

_____   _____

p _____   _____

_____   _____

q _____   _____

_____   _____

r _____   _____

_____   _____

s _____   _____

_____   _____

t _____   _____

_____   _____

u _____   _____

_____   _____

v _____   _____

_____   _____

w _____   _____

_____   _____

x _____   _____

   _____   _____

y _____   _____

   _____   _____

z _____   _____

   _____   _____

Another fun, interesting way to present beginning phonetic sounds to your toddler is to introduce an object such as a bat. Then say to the child, "Bat begins with a 'b.' Other words that begin with 'b' are *boy, bus, bar,* and *bike*." If you don't have all of the objects available, that's okay; just say the words. Pay attention to your delivery. Make sure the "b" sounds are clear and distinct. Pop the "b" through your lips with a fast, hard, short breath. Feel it supported by your diaphragm. It will sound like *bah*.

Present as many real objects to the child as possible (e.g., basket of fruit, vegetables, tools, etc.). This enables the child to experience the concrete meaning of the word through the senses visually (this is red or blue), tactilely (this is rough or smooth), thermally (this is hot or cold), barically (this is heavy or light), gustatorally (this is sweet or sour), olfactorily (this is floral or pungent), auditorily (this is loud or soft), and stereognostically (covering the eyes to heighten all other senses and form a visual image of an object).

Think about a head of lettuce. It has beautiful color and a smooth texture; it is cool and wet to the touch and smells fresh. It also allows the child to gain tactile strength and concentration by pulling apart the leaves one by one. Let the child taste it. To a child, this experience is a drink of life. Remember, young children see with their hands and mouths.

> *Remember, young children see with their hands and mouths.*

It isn't always practical or possible to introduce real objects to a child, but you'll be amazed at the "real-looking" miniature objects that are available for purchase at cake-decorating stores (e.g., horse, flute, drum, golf club, carousel, violin, etc.).

Make sure these objects look as true to life as possible. Instead of a solid purple dinosaur, present one to the child that replicates the colors of a real dinosaur. This way, you will be presenting one concept only. If you show a solid purple dinosaur, the child's impression will be that all dinosaurs are purple. If you show the object to the child and say "purple," guess what? The child will think that the color purple is shaped like a dinosaur.

As a basic rule of thumb, present one concept at a time. Choose either objects or colors.

Language Presentation Exercises

1. Sit in front of the child with a basket or pillow-case of objects in your lap. Keep the objects close to you. This controls the child's impulse to grab for them.

2. Pick an object out of the basket. Hold it in your hand for a moment. Make sure it's eye level to the child. If the child is distracted, you can ask, "Where are your eyes?" Sometimes, I will tap the outer corner of my eye to gain the child's visual attention.

3. *Slow . . . down . . . your . . . speech.* Crisply enunciate beginning, middle, and ending sounds in all words. You'll make it easier for the child to understand what you're saying, and you'll help the child communicate thoughts and feelings earlier.

4. Wait for the child to emulate you. Remember to be silent and patient. If the child reaches for the object, let him hold it. Once the child's tactile and visual craving has been satisfied, give the auditory presentation.

It may take several presentations before the child can say the word, or you might hear only part of it, like the "aaa" when you present "cat." Do not expect too much too soon. If you constantly correct or become impatient, the child will sense your frustration. He may stop trying to speak, leading to shyness, insecurity, stuttering, and regular visits to the speech pathologist later on. Silence is a precious commodity you can give the child whose fledgling words are learning to fly (see chapter 5).

Now your fifteen-month-old says "aaa" after you present the word "cat." Present the word again. If the child still says "aaa," the physical structures to articulate the "c" might not be in place yet. There is also the possibility that the child can say the "c" with a little prompting from you. Say the word again using letter-by-letter slow motion. Say "c-a-t." Make sure you emphasize each sound clearly. If the child reaches with you to enunciate all of the letters, keep repeating the word. If you start to feel tension and resistance, stop and go onto the next object. Remember, you want this to be fun for both of you.

Never correct the child while he is attempting to say the word.

Never correct the child while he is attempting to say the word. Repeat the word for clarification once more before you put the object back into the basket. Keep your eyes on "next time."

Keep the objects available for the child's exploration. It is important that the baskets are placed on a shelf that is eye level to the child, or on small (eighteen-inch-square) work rugs. This visually emphasizes where the activities are and where they belong when your toddler is finished. Make these interesting activ- ity centers available to the child in every room to which he has access. Rotate the objects and introduce new ones to continually challenge the child. Make sure to keep the objects out at least thirty days to ensure each new concept is internalized by the child.

You will notice that I have not given specific age requirements for what your child should accomplish. He will determine the pace. It's the emotional environment, physical and mental stimulation, and nature's will (the formation of bodily structures for speech) that determine a child's linguistic development.

Make a list of beginning phonetic sounds and words presented to your toddler.

Sound d___   Sound _____

Words___dog_____   Words _____

___dish_____   _____

Sound _____   Sound _____

Words_____   Words _____

_____   _____

_____   _____

Sound _____   Sound _____

Words_____   Words _____

_____   _____

_____   _____

Sound _____   Sound _____

Words_____   Words _____

_____   _____

_____   _____

Creating Activities That Advance Concentration, Verbal, and Fine Motor Skills

Gather real objects from the environment such as a watch, screwdriver, sunglasses, ring, calculator, etc. into a large basket. A cloth bag or pillowcase works well, too, because you can take objects out of the bag without the visual distraction of the other objects.

When you have enough objects, start categorizing them. For example, put farm animals, insects, flowers, etc. into individual baskets.

You can also look through magazines and find pictures that correspond to various objects in a basket. Cut them out and secure them to card stock, leaving one side blank. Then laminate for durability. Give a presentation on how to match the objects to their corresponding pictures. Using a work rug, begin with matching three insects.

Slowly line the cards one by one in the middle of the rug, from left to right, horizontally. Place objects on the left side of the rug in a similar fashion. (Setting up exercises that train the child to work from left to right strengthens the eye muscles with the left-to-right eye swoop, remote preparation for reading.) Slowly pick up one object, pause, and look at the child. This process will keep you connected to the child and (if you smile) create a fun and enjoyable learning environment.

Move the object from one picture to the next with great deliberation until you place it on the corresponding picture. After you match all of the objects to the pictures, slowly, one by one, put all objects and pictures back into the basket. This helps the child sequence and develop organizational skills. Then say to the child, "You match them now." Get up and let the child do the work. Make a concerted effort not to disturb or correct him while he is concentrating.

Make sure when the child is finished working that the objects and pictures are placed back into the basket. You may have to re-demonstrate and put a few of the cards and objects back into the basket for him. Amazingly, once the child sees you putting the cards and objects back into the basket, he will want to complete the full cycle of the activity (prepare the work area and put the work away) without you.

Once the toddler has mastered the concept of matching objects to the correct pictures, then you may present the language. A good way to present language is to say the name of the object as you are putting it into the basket. This may be a day or a week later. Increase the number of objects and cards to challenge the child. Stay within the format of working from left to right by increasing the number of rows horizontally.

Another idea is to put pictures of various people, places, and things that represent our culture (and other cultures) in categorical baskets. Show the pictures to the toddler, then give the word (for example, *mountain, lake, stream, canyon,* etc.). Start with three cards and place them neatly from left to right on a small carpet. Increase the number of pictures to add a challenge to the exercise. Lining up cards neatly on the carpet reinforces precision and organization in the child's thinking. The goal of the exercise is enrichment of vocabulary, concentration, coordination, and self-control.

Be creative. When the child becomes adept at matching various objects with similar pictures and can sequence them on a rug, design matching activities that require a bit more concentration and logic (abstracting). For example, use objects such as swordfish, Chevrolet, rose, hummingbird, etc. Match them to pictures that are in the same category, but are not exactly the same. For example, match swordfish to trout, Chevrolet to Buick, rose to daffodil, and hummingbird to cardinal. Another challenging exercise for children is to match pictures of people together. There are games such as "President's Lotto" where children match individual pictures of presidents to their corresponding photographs on a game card. You can make up your own lotto cards. Make sure the cards in the matching exercise challenge the child to work from left to right.

Make booklets for the child. Take photographs of one object at a time. Enlarge, laminate, then secure them together.

Make photographs into slides and project them onto the wall. Find postcards and cut pictures out of magazines. The bigger the picture, the better. What you present to the child competes with the vastness of stimuli all around.

When presenting a new concept to the child, be sure to isolate one idea at a time.

1. **Rabbit**—Make sure the picture is a "real" rabbit, not Bugs Bunny. Have nothing else in the picture except a rabbit.

2. **Lamp**—Show the picture of a lamp only, not one sitting on a table.

3. **Peninsula**—Show a close-up of how the land protrudes into the ocean. Make sure no islands or ships are in the water.

Similarly, it is important that the young child's first experience of quantities (numbers) is as concrete as possible. Abstractions will come soon enough. For example, place one apricot on the table in front of the child and say, "One." Put another apricot next to it and say, "Two." Let the child hold the two apricots. Place another apricot on the table and say, "Three." Let the child explore and experience three apricots. Take one apricot away and say, "Three apricots take away one makes two." Once the child has mastered the concept of three apricots, introduce three more. This is a richer, fuller learning experience than looking at numbers on a blackboard that say 1+1=2; 2+1=3; 3-1=2; etc.

Another example of a concrete learning experience would be going to the petting zoo with the child and introducing a rabbit. First, the child sees it (visual sense), feels it (tactile sense), and smells it (olfactory sense). This is a sensory extravaganza for the toddler. The toddler's eyes light up as the inexplicable gentleness of life passes through his delicate arms and soul, touching a place that a cartoon rendering of Bugs Bunny could never find.

Continually present new concepts to the child. Take the child with you wherever you go. Immerse him in his culture. When you're at home, find new ways to enrich the child's life through challenging physical and mental modes of activity.

Material-making ideas for my toddler's enjoyment and development:

Activity   ***Picture Matching***

Materials   **Calendar** with large pictures of individual breeds of dogs displayed monthly

Dog magazine containing pictures of

individual breeds of dogs similar to the

calendar

Scissors

Poster board (card stock)

Glue stick

Laminator or laminating paper

Activity ***Coin Matching—Object to Picture***

Materials **Pennies, nickels, dimes, quarters,**

fifty-cent pieces

Currency book

Scissors

Poster board (card stock)

Glue stick

Laminator or laminating paper

Activity

Materials

_____

_____

_____

_____

Activity   _____

Materials   _____

_____

_____

_____

_____

Activity   _____

Materials   _____

_____

_____

_____

_____

Enrichment and Expression of Vocabulary through Toddler-Appropriate Literature

Read books with your toddler. Make sure the books you present are appropriate to hold the child's interest. Find books with little or no text and large realistic pictures.

These books are hard to find. It's important that the child not be overstimulated by too many words or pictures at once. Always pause and look into the child's eyes as you read. This helps to keep the child's interest and lengthens his periods of concentration.

Chunky board books are wonderful for toddlers. A few recommendations published by Simon Juvenile are *In the Garden, In the Bathroom,* and *Family Time. Mrs. Mustard's Baby Faces* and *Animals A–Z,* published by Chronicle Books, are also toddler-appropriate. Another personal favorite, published by Bantam Books, is *Jamberry.* Though the pictures are cartoon renderings, they are simple and true to life. The music in the words will captivate and entertain the child day after day. Fiona Pragoff's *Autumn, Summer, Winter,* and *Fall* are exquisite picture books, as well.

Toddlers, as well as young children, absolutely adore the Crozat series of animal books, including *I*

Always pause and look into the child's eyes as you read.

Am a Little Monkey, I Am a Little Duck, and *I Am a Little Dinosaur.* The illustrations are not real photographs, but they capture the essence of life with real emotions expressed through the animals. They are impeccably drawn and true to form. The scenes of natural habitats are colorful and inviting with little visual surprises tastefully presented to enrich, not overwhelm, the child's visual experience. The reason these books work for young children (older as well) is because of the repetition of the scenes and the minimal text.

I usually make up my own story if a book is too wordy for the child. If he starts squirming, disregard the words and turn the page. Use buzzwords that the child can relate to, such as *mother, father, family, brother, sister, drink of water, eat bananas,* etc.

Deep emotion and exaggerated facial expressions will attract the child's attention immediately. One of my favorite picture books to read to toddlers is *Grandpa's Face,* by Eloise Greenfield. Not only are the large illustrations appealing to the toddler, but there isn't much text. The emotion in the character's eyes is extremely appealing to the child who is just recognizing feelings.

Modify the story to the child's attention span. Observe and recognize when you are losing his interest. Once again, use words or phrases from the text that are familiar to the child.

I also like to show pictures of children who are happy, sad, afraid, frustrated, proud, or angry. These pictures and books are found in teachers' stores. Showing these pictures to your toddler may evoke his expression of feelings to you ("Yeah, I was angry, too" or "The lightning and thunder scared me"). Always support the child in verbally expressing his feelings.

The *Fit-a-Shape* book series published by Quarto Children's Books is also very nice. Your toddler needs to have fairly good hand-eye coordination to put them together. Keep these books on hand, as they could challenge his fine motor development.

When demonstrating how to fit shapes into a book or puzzle, the child should sit on your left. (If you are left-handed, the child should sit on your right.) This way, the child can always see what the active hand is doing. Show the child how to manipulate each shape into its corresponding space. Deliberately slow down your movements so the child can analyze what you are doing. Hold the puzzle piece directly over each empty space and position it several ways before placing it into the correct slot. By doing this, you will be modeling reasoning, comparing, patience, and exactness. Refrain from talking. Be cognizant of your use of two actions: talking and showing.

Use puzzles with little knobs attached to the puzzle pieces. These are easier for your toddler to handle, building muscle strength in his first three fingers and preparing him for writing.

Once the child is skilled at holding a puzzle piece by the knob, you can create tracing exercises on plain paper using a pencil. Find puzzles with geometric shapes, animals, or objects that are easy for your fledgling writer to trace.

Modeling Language to Support Your Toddler's Concentration Skills

To inspire language development in the child who is hesitant or not yet speaking audible sounds, find verbal techniques that will attract the child's attention. Constantly yelling or talking too fast will repel the child's interest in language. In fact, he'll quickly go into auditory overload and won't hear you. Slowing down your speech and using clear articulation and a low, gentle tone will attract the toddler like a butterfly to nectar, even when you're setting limits. As general guidelines, you should look deeply into the child's eyes and use simple language that describes frame-by-frame and word-for-word objects and actions relating to the child's immediate experience.

For example, before serving snack I say, "We are having a snack." While putting down the napkin I show the child the napkin and say, "Napkin." Then I hand a cracker to the child and say, "Cracker." I sit down across from the child and eat my snack. After chewing a bite of cracker, I say, "I'm eating my cracker." After the child and I are finished with our snacks, I get up and throw my napkin and cup into the trash. Ideally, the child will emulate me.

There will be added challenges in the child's home environment. For example, your child has taken one bite out of a cracker and the dog runs into the room. Your child gets up and chases the dog into the living room, still eating the cracker. While getting up, he knocks over a glass of juice. The number-one priority is redirecting the child's focus back to the original activity, which was eating a snack. Walk over, look into your child's eyes and whisper, "I sit with my cracker." Say no more. Hold out your hand to the child and lead him back to the table.

Singing is a powerful device to help your child stay focused. You might even make up a little melody as you lead him to the table. Example, "I sit with my

cracker, my cracker, my cracker. I sit with my cracker
. . ." and so forth. Always keep in mind the explosive
nature of stimuli versus the toddler's concentration.

Now, we are back at the table and your child
steps in the apple juice that was spilled on the floor.
Remember, one thing at a time. The most important
action right now (since you have been singing about
it) is for your child to sit, even if there's apple juice
on the floor. Look into his eyes and say, "I sit while I
eat my cracker." When the child is finished eating,
point to the spill and say, "Look, it's apple juice."
Touch it and invite the child to touch it. Say, "Feel.
Wet. Let's clean it up." Have sponges or a child-sized
mop available to wipe up spills. Your child will want
to help clean up to the best of his ability.

Now, it's time to put our things away. I say, "I take
my cup to the trash." I use first person ("I take," "I
am," etc.) so the child not only hears the words, but
identifies with the "I." We are giving the child the
words for what is happening in his life at the
moment. This shows synchronicity, the mind and
body working together. You're orchestrating and wit-
nessing your child's early glimpses of concentration.
What a gift it is to help him develop mental hardware
that enables him to stay focused and complete pro-

jects. Crossing t's, dotting i's, and putting periods at the ends of sentences will be a given for this child.

As far as language goes, your child might not be able to say words or phrases yet, but he still feels connected and centered in our loving support and intent to help him make sense of it all. This is very calming and satisfying to your toddler. The child has the same amount of life energy and emotion inside that you do (oh, maybe a little more) without the practical experience or technical skills to define or express them in a language that we understand. Sadly, we sometimes jump to conclusions and grossly misjudge the toddler's behavior and intentions. It's up to us as caregivers to empower our children with assertive speech and good listening skills. This includes respecting and honoring the child's physical and emotional boundaries, which will be discussed in chapter 2.

Sadly, we sometimes jump to conclusions and grossly misjudge the toddler's behavior and intentions.

The ability to honestly communicate is the greatest gift we can bestow upon our children as they enter the mainstream of our culture. Yes, this begins in infancy (even in the womb) and can be realized as the child enters into the third year of life. In fact, this wonderfully assertive child will continue to pursue this powerful habit into adolescence, reaching for the right word rather than oppressing feelings, which would likely cause destructive behavior later on.

Notes _____

_____

_____

_____

_____

_____

_____

_____

_____

_____

_____

2 Honoring Your Toddler's Physical and Emotional Boundaries

Tantrums No More

What would it feel like not to be able to tell the doctor what hurts, honk the horn at the guy who's about to cut you off in traffic, tell your neighbor to keep his dog out of your vegetable garden, or ask your son to replace the thousand-dollar fender he just smashed into a telephone pole? How would you feel? Probably like dumping your food or pushing and hitting someone. Maybe it would feel better to pull hair, yours or someone else's!

Funny, when a *child* exhibits these physical displays of emotion, we call them "tantrums." When *we* kick a tire, throw a pencil, or slam a door, we're simply "angry" or "frustrated." Think about this. Instead of labeling the child's behavior as a tantrum, think of him as simply expressing anger or frustration in the only language available at the moment—"toddler language."

The child probably is upset because someone or something invaded a very personal and important physical or emotional boundary. Please keep in mind that the child doesn't have an appropriate vehicle of self-expression. Instead of punishing or shaming the child for being upset, sit with him. Try to identify and acknowledge the feeling behind the child's behavior, whether it's throwing a toy, hitting you, biting a friend, crying, etc. Whatever the physical expression, it's just a symptom of what's going on, not the cause. This is where you can really become the child's ally and not get caught up in power struggles.

Whatever the physical expression, it's just a symptom of what's going on, not the cause.

Once the child has calmed down and can look into your eyes, say, "I see you're frustrated or angry." After you acknowledge your child's feelings, ask, "Can you say, 'I'm mad'?" Then ask him to say it again, louder this time. If you can model the use of language to express anger, you can give the child an invaluable release. Believe me, it feels a lot better for your child to exclaim "I'm mad!" than to fall down on the kitchen floor and start kicking. As soon as you acknowledge his feelings, you will have a friend for life.

If this is a very young toddler who can't articulate "I'm mad," say it for him. Look into the child's eyes and say several times, "I'm mad." Say it softer to louder. The toddler will experience a cathartic release through you. I really believe that the toddler is experiencing a great deal of fear as well as anger when physically out of control. It physiologically resembles a seizure and uses a lot of emotional and physical energy. Now, we put on our detective hats. What happened? This is more important than the child's hysteria.

Four Steps to Resolving Emotional Conflict

1. Acknowledge Feelings

"I see you're mad, sad, frustrated, hurt, concentrating, happy, etc." Be empathetic to the child's feelings, but be swift to empower the child with tools of resolution. Too much empathy can turn into maudlin sympathy, which can develop into an unhealthy dependence on you.

2. Put on Your Detective Hat

Find out what happened. For example, "Did Joey take something from you?" "Did you fall from the slide?" "Are you frustrated because you need help finishing the puzzle?" "Did I put your shoes on in haste when you wanted to dress yourself?"

As a detective, you also will learn to avoid personal conflict with your toddler by thinking about the potential consequences of your actions. Always relate to the child using techniques that produce peaceful and harmonious results. This takes lots of self-control, experimentation, and practice. There are many cases in which you will put on your detective hat before you even approach the child.

3. Explain Why

If you caused the upset, "explain why" to the child. For example, "I'm late for work," "I lost my patience," or "I'm not in a very good mood." If another child is involved, resolve the conflict fairly with both children present (see page 41). For example, "Billy, you must have been mad to have hit Ellen," or "Joey, Brian really wants the dinosaur. May he play with it when you are through?" (Then you support Brian in asking for a turn when Joey is finished with it.)

4. Give Choices That Lead to a Win-Win Resolution

If you caused the upset, give choices that will make all parties involved happy. For example, "You can play for five more minutes and then we have to go," or "I'll help you put on your right shoe. You put on the left shoe." If another child is involved in the conflict, create a resolution where everyone wins. For example, "Stephen, let's play a patience game until Kayla is through playing with the train." (Then you get a set of keys or something interesting and take turns holding it with Stephen.)

Try practicing this four-step process once a week as it relates to your own family situation.

My toddler: did not want to get off of the swing and come home from preschool with me.

I used to respond: by raising my voice several times, then demanding he come home with me, now!

My toddler used to respond: by ignoring me, then raising his voice at me, shouting, "No!"

I used to respond: by physically removing him from the swing.

My toddler used to respond: by hitting and kicking.

My new response is to acknowledge feelings: "I see you're having a wonderful time on the swing."

Put on my detective hat: I know he won't want to come with me right away. He'll get upset if I try to rush him.

Explain why: "I'm a little short on time today. We have to stop and pick up a few things for dinner."

Give choices that lead to a win-win resolution: "I'll sit and watch you swing for three more minutes. Then we need to go to the store. Will you help me pick out a good dessert?"

My toddler: is potty training and will not go into the bathroom with me to try and urinate.

I used to respond: by reminding him (sternly) of the accidents he already had that day.

My toddler used to respond: by saying, "No, I don't have to go."

I used to respond: by physically taking my son into the bathroom and pulling down his pants.

My toddler used to respond: by urinating on himself and on the floor.

My new response is to acknowledge feelings: "I know how important your work is. I waited until you were finished with the puzzle."

Put on my detective hat: I want to make this a positive, pleasurable experience—maybe even have a little fun.

Explain why: "It's been awhile since we went to the bathroom. Let's go see if our bladders are empty or full. It's better for us when they're empty."

Give choices that lead to a win-win resolution: Do you want to go first or should I?

My toddler:

I used to respond:

My toddler used to respond:

_____

_____

I used to respond: _____

_____

My toddler used to respond: _____

_____

_____

My new response is to acknowledge feelings: ___

_____

_____

_____

Put on my detective hat: _____

_____

_____

_____

Explain why: _____

_____

_____

_____

Give choices that lead to a win-win resolution: _____

_____

_____

Ten Ways to Avoid Emotional Conflict

1. Resolve Conflicts Fairly

Suppose Joey is crying because Kenny, Joey's older brother, took a truck from him. Invite Kenny and Joey to accompany you to a place where the three of you can resolve the conflict in private. This will ensure that you're not shaming Kenny in front of his friends. You may not be clear about what happened but, you may be able to discern that Kenny did something to Joey.

Put on your detective hat. Ask Kenny what happened. Believe me, Kenny already knows he did

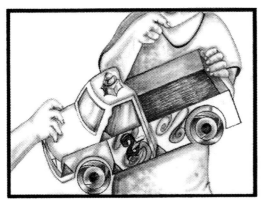

something wrong. In fact, he might give Joey the truck back on the spot. If he does, do not say anything more! The conflict is resolved. Trust that it was enough that you removed Kenny from his friends and the play area. The consequence is built into the outcome. He no longer has the truck.

To verbally reprimand him is to discount his graciousness in giving the truck back and he will equate doing the right thing with still being wrong. A "thumbs-up" gesture or gentle touch will affirm his correct action. Always examine your own motives and reactions and make sure these situations don't become a forum for expressing your anger at having your card game interrupted. *Having children = Having interruptions.*

Worst case scenario: Kenny is holding onto the truck with all his might. Joey walks over to him and tries to take the truck back. They become physical.

In an assertive voice ask, "Words! Where are your words?" Bend down to the children's eye level and make deep eye contact. Continue in a calmer tone of voice, saying, "I don't like to see you hurting each other. You are precious children." Kenny may say that he had wanted the truck or he had it first, or he may say, "NO!" This is when Mom or Dad's intuition really comes in.

Usually the child who is the most upset during the resolution process is the one who's been violated. (However, there are always exceptions.) If both are equally upset, continue with your resolution attempt. Keep your detective hat on. Answers will come as you spend more time with the children. Watch body language, etc. One of the children might see something he'd rather play with and walk away. At that point, the conflict is over. No sense dragging the child (who has found interest elsewhere) back to resolve the conflict. Then you'll be resolving a new conflict, because he's already forgotten about the incident and is probably fixated on a new activity. Besides, Joey's happy because he has the truck. When there's peace, don't fix it!

If Kenny is still clutching onto the truck he took from Joey, encourage Joey to look into Kenny's eyes, hold out his hand and ask, "May I have it?" If Joey is

> *Usually the child who is the most upset during the resolution process is the one who's been violated.*

not capable of using words, help him to hold out his hand and you ask for him, "May I have it?" We are the living examples. Always resolve conflicts with respect and dignity.

If the child doesn't give it back, acknowledge his feelings. Say, "I know it's hard for you to give the truck back." Then explain why: "Joey did have it first." If Kenny still does not relinquish the truck, give him a choice. Hold out your hand and say, "Give the truck to Joey or to me." Odds are Kenny will give the truck to you. (He still needs one more outlet to display his frustration at having to relinquish the truck. Who knows how many times Joey or Kenny's older friends have taken things from him?)

Okay, let's say Kenny still hasn't given the truck back. Start counting in a firm voice, "One, two, three." This usually works, but if you need a last resort, say in a stern voice, "I'm getting angry!" Look into Kenny's eyes. "I want you to give the truck back to Joey or I'll help you give it back to him." At this point you might even interest Kenny in another activity. Your consideration of both children will demonstrate fairness (win-win) in conflict resolution. But . . . you might have to assist Kenny in giving back the truck by gently guiding Kenny's arms (which are clinging to the truck) in Joey's direction. Help with the release of the truck. Remember, you have given Kenny choice after choice and he has chosen your assistance.

Usually the conflict will be resolved and Kenny won't be upset after he gives back the truck because he innately knows he was inappropriate. However, if Kenny does get upset (and this does happen once in awhile), it might mean that he really didn't take the truck from Joey after all. Maybe Joey tried to take it from him and Kenny pushed him. If you're at a loss as to what happened and feel you made a mistake as a detective, it's okay. What I usually say is, "Look, I made a mistake. Tell you what, since I wasn't here and didn't see what happened, I'll just take the truck. Maybe tomorrow you'll both be able to play with it nicely."

Note: I am attempting to cover all possibilities so you will have many options during conflict resolution.

Even if what you assumed was wrong, you have set an example by negotiating fairly. You have modeled assertive behavior to the children and used appropriate language to demonstrate that. Before you know it, you won't ever be involved in the conflict. Joey will learn how to ask for the truck back and Kenny will remember that giving it back is a pleasurable experience. **This does not happen overnight. Be prepared to demonstrate conflict resolution over, over, and over again.** Toddlers and young children are just learning the concept of boundaries, and with a toddler, everything is his!

Pat yourself on the back after modeling conflict resolution. With Kenny, you took the time to acknowledge feelings and explain. You gave him choices. Then you gave him a consequence by helping him to relinquish the truck. Once Kenny experiences where limits are and that there are concrete consequences for his behavior, the next time he will give the truck back to Joey. He doesn't enjoy the tension any more than you do.

Important note: I am sharing dialogue and conflict resolution styles that have worked for me with most children. Some children respond differently. For example, they might need to know "why" they need to do something before you acknowledge their feelings. Nothing is etched in stone as far as sequence is concerned. Keep trying until you find what works.

Always follow through with consequences when you set a limit. The toddler really wants you to keep your word. Following through on limits and consequences means:

- loving the child

- differentiating between appropriate and inappropri-ate behavior

- having a conscience

- teaching respect for others

- promoting self-discipline and self-respect

Supporting the resolution of a conflict with your time, fairness, and emotional availability helps the child develop empathy, tenacity, and concentration.

2. Respect Your Child's Concentration

Imagine this: You're working on *The New York Times* crossword puzzle. You're just about to solve it and a giant interrupts your train of thought and says to you, "Okay, Susan, put the puzzle away. We're going." Five more words and you've solved the puzzle. Now the giant's voice is even louder. "Susan, put the puzzle away.

WE'RE GOING!" Now you're feeling tense. You've forgotten the correct answer that you just remembered. Pressure and frustration are mounting. Now the giant is standing over you and grabs *The New York Times* out of your hands and screams, "NOW!" How would you feel? Personally, I might feel like drop-kicking the giant! Especially if I didn't have the words to assertively express my anger with the giant's discounting and demanding approach.

Now, let's replay that scene with a "best case" outcome. I'm working on *The New York Times* puzzle, just about to solve it and in deep concentration. No one interrupts me. Finally, it's solved. Wow . . . I feel great! I feel a sense of relief and victory at the same time. Then I smile and revel in my accomplishment. My self-esteem goes up at least five notches. And the best part is, I did it myself! I'm competent, capable, tenacious, knowledgeable, and I learned four new words in the challenge of solving the puzzle. I'm growing, expanding, stretching, learning, and becoming . . . I can do it!

Second-best outcome: I'm working on *The New York Times* puzzle. Just about to solve it. I'm in deep concentration. A giant walks into the room and stands quietly by the door. I continue to concentrate. *Hmmm, I know that word. It's on the tip of my tongue.* The giant is still there and sits down quietly. (Acting like a detective, assessing the most respectful time to approach me.) Back to the puzzle. Then I try it from another angle; *24 across is . . . let's see.* I reach for the thesaurus and knock the newspaper on the floor. As I pick up the newspaper, the giant walks over to me and whispers, "I see you're really concentrating on the puzzle." (Acknowledging my feelings.) "I'm sorry to interrupt you, but you have a dentist appointment in one hour." (Telling me why.) "Do you need a few more minutes or can you finish it when we come back?" (Giving me a choice.)

Let's say I really wanted a few more minutes. The giant leaves the room. I continue working on the puzzle. In five minutes, the giant comes back into the room and gently reminds me that it's time to go. After all, five more minutes working on the puzzle was my choice, so of course I'll comply graciously. But if I'm a little short on sleep, I might not.

The consequential outcome: The giant says, "Okay, I'm getting angry. We had an agreement and you're breaking it. Either you come with me now, or I'll help you to come with me." The giant holds out a hand, looks deeply into my eyes and says, "Come, please." Whew! Of course I'll comply. This giant has taken the time to make me feel important. The giant

also made me feel like what I was doing was important, that my feelings are important, that my teeth and
keeping a commitment are also important. Sounds
like win-win to me!

3. Always Ask, "May I?"

Value and cherish the child by continually
demonstrating and verbalizing respectful
communication. Always ask before you
touch anything your child has in hand,
whether it be a crumb picked up from the
kitchen floor or a lamb chop taken off
a platter. Ask, "May I have this?" (Do not
touch!)

Simplify or enrich the language depend-
ing on the child's verbal skills. For the child
who is just beginning to use words, ask,
"May I?" Then hold out your hand. Your body
language will reinforce that you are request-
ing the object. Asking "May I?" respects the
child's feelings by giving him control of the
object in hand and the right to say "No."

Let's say the child has a piece of cake in his
hand that he picked up off of the floor.
Acknowledge his feelings by saying, "Joey, I know it's
hard for you not to eat this cake." Now, explain why.
(Use concerned, loving eye contact.) Say, "I don't

want you to eat this cake because it's been on the floor. Germs are there." You can even make a face when saying "germs." "Please throw the cake in the trash. We'll get another piece." This technique has never failed. It is more difficult for younger children or children who are determined (cake-a-holics). In these instances, modify language. Get to the point and resolution quicker. For example, "Stop! Germs. Trash. Fresh piece."

Important note: No matter what verbal skills the child is or isn't demonstrating and whether or not the child fully comprehends your words, he will intuitively feel and understand your loving intent. Use repetition and patience. One day when you least expect it, you won't have to say a word. (Yes, even at twenty-two months old.) The child will drop a piece of cake on the floor, pick it up, look at you, say "germs," make a face, miraculously toss it into the trash, then ask for a fresh piece.

If you want to demonstrate to the child how to do something (build with blocks or put a puzzle together) wait until there is a break in the child's concentration. Ask, "May I?" or "May I show you?" Make sure you look at the child, pause and give him time to answer. If the child says "no," then back off! **Children have the right to say no**. The more you honor that

Once the child trusts and internalizes that his space and rights are being honored, you'll get compliance and respect in return.

right, the more times you'll hear "yes." The longer the child has felt personal boundary violations, the more times you'll hear "no." You'll even get a no if the child wants to say yes. This child needs to say no and be respected. Once the child trusts and internalizes that his space and rights are being honored, you'll get compliance and respect in return. A caged bird sings the song that's sung to it.

If you make a mistake and the toddler perceives a personal boundary violation, amends are always an option. What a divine example of humility and human fallibility. Apologies are important for the toddler to experience. The same formula for conflict resolution is appropriate in this case. Say, "I see your feelings are hurt." (Acknowledgment) "I'm sorry I spoke unkindly to you." (Detective hat) "I guess I'm a little rushed this morning." (Why) "Do you want one last bite of the cereal or the bagel?" (Choice) "I promise that we'll have more time to eat breakfast tomorrow." (Resolution)

If you have been consistent with the fair, respectful, and equitable approach in most situations, a mistake once in awhile will be easily forgotten. If the toddler has felt violated time and time again, be patient. The child's sense of feeling hurt might be stronger than his sense of feeling honored. A mistake could trigger painful memories to surface along with the learned response of expressing anger and frustration through physical displays of emotion (hitting, biting, etc.). Don't react angrily. (Your behavior is contagious to the child.) Refer back to your new techniques of responding to the child who is upset. This could be one more test your toddler has developed to get reassurance that he will be respected.

The healing of your relationship has begun; two richer, fuller human beings emerge in the midst of turmoil and change. A new intimacy and trust evolves.

People who love children change the world by changing themselves.

4. Wipe and Blow Little Noses Gently

Imagine you are sitting in your favorite chair, listening to Beethoven and relaxing from a long, busy day. Your nose starts running and suddenly, without warning, someone reaches from behind and pinches your nostrils with a tissue. Surprise! But once is not enough. Here comes the pincers again, with a vengeance.

This time you try and protect yourself from the assailant. You turn your head. The perpetrator, who is bigger and stronger than you, waits until you turn your head back again. Before you know it, your already-sensitive nose is in the vice-like grip again. You try to get away. Either way, you lose: If you move, you'll get a nose job without anesthesia, and if you remain still, your nose will be squeezed and probed relentlessly.

Life would have been so much easier and less irritating if you were given the responsibility of wiping your own nose.

Caregivers, hear this:

- The child is resistant to your nose-wiping overture because previous experiences with your technique have not been pleasant ones.

- You are interrupting the child's concentration.

- You are taking control of the child's body.

- You are projecting your abhorrence of nasal discharge and your need to see perfect nasal cleanliness—now!

As soon as your child can hold a tissue, he is ready to learn how to wipe and blow his own nose. Sit in front of the child with a box of tissues. Make sure it's out of his reach. Slowly pull out a tissue. Put the tissue on the table or floor. Pause and look at the child. Fold the tissue in half.

Note: The fewer fine motor skills the child has, the fewer steps you should use.

Pick up the folded tissue with two hands and place the tissue over your nose. Blow, then wipe. Bring hands together while removing the tissue from your nose to indicate a gentle pinching gesture. Place the box of tissues in front of the child. Say, "Your turn." Let the child emulate you. Don't make any faces of disgust if there is mucus on the child's face. Ask in a loving way, "May I help you?" Then, gently wipe the child's nose and face. The child will begin to trust you. Next, get up and deposit the soiled tissue into the trash. Encourage the child to do the same.

If the child is busy working on a project and you notice mucus is everywhere, at the appropriate time (when the child takes a break from concentrating), without saying a word, demonstrate nose wiping and blowing.

Hand the box of tissues to the child. If the child needs help, always ask, "May I help you?" If the child's experience with nose wiping and blowing has been a pleasant one, the child will always comply. If he does not, be patient. You may have to regain trust and live with an imperfect nose-wiping job a little longer.

Runny noses are synonymous with toddlerhood. Always keep a box of tissues within the child's reach. Empower the child to take control of his own body. Yes, two-year-olds are perfectly capable of wiping and blowing their own noses.

Note: You may present simple language to the child using words like *runny nose, tissue, wipe*, and *trash*. Make sure these words are given after the nose wiping and blowing demonstration, remembering to separate the visual and auditory lessons you give to the child.

5. Support Your Child's Bathroom Independence

First weaning, then walking, and now the toddler enters another important phase of development: bathroom independence.

When and how do caregivers support (not stifle) this process?

The ideal situation starts in infancy with the use of cloth diapers or training pants, which encourages the child to stay associated with the feeling of urination and having a bowel movement. Unfortunately, this has become a society of mega-absorbency paper diapers and pull-ups that promote the disassociation of the child from bodily functions. So an important first step would be to introduce the child to training pants.

It is a mixed message when we are supporting the child's independence and at the same time requiring him to come to the adult to tie his shoes.

Just as instrumental as training pants is the child's involvement in self-care. This can begin with the infant who pulls the training pants out of a drawer and continues with the toddler who is gaining the skills to dress and undress.

Always dress the toddler who is striving for bathroom independence in clothes that are loose and can be taken off and put on easily. Make sure shoes can be secured and unsecured by the child. It is a mixed message when we are supporting the child's independence and at the same time requiring him to come to the adult to tie his shoes. Slip-ons and Velcro shoes are wonderful for the toddler.

Let the child set the pace for how little or how much support is needed during this process. I have learned subtle ways to assist the toddler in gaining control of his body for self-care.

A few hints:

- For the child who needs help focusing on the task at hand, eliminate distractions such as having to deal with all of the clothes at once—make available only one item, i.e., training pants. Then once the child has put on the training pants, lay out the shorts, then the socks, etc.

- Lay out the shorts in front of the child in a manner that "shows" the two openings for each leg. This keeps the child from fumbling with a rolled-up pair of pants and continually putting two legs into one opening.

- Never correct the child who is trying to dress and ends up with pants inside out and shoes on the wrong feet. This can be corrected in fifteen minutes, when the child does not associate the failed attempt with his Herculean effort.

- Be sensitive to the timing of a gentle reminder. When it's time for a bathroom break or a change, always respect the child's concentration.

Every child has a different timetable when it comes to bathroom independence. If you try to force the issue on "getting it" as fast as his older sister, you will set the stage for struggle and frustration. Take the child with you to the bathroom. Have older siblings invite the child to the bathroom with them. Example is the greatest teacher.

If you are supporting the child's bathroom independence and still using diapers, this is extremely confusing to the toddler. Diapers are a powerful symbol of infancy and dependency. Have a celebration (rite of passage) in which you throw away all of the diapers. The toddler is no longer an infant.

Most important of all is to stay positive, even when there is a bowel movement sliding down the toddler's leg, or when you're assisting in changing soiled clothing. Eliminate the phrases "I smell poop," "Yuck," "Something smells terrible," and "You're dirty." Replace all negative connotations with positive: "It smells like you've had a bowel movement," or "Let's put on fresh clothes." This positive response to your child's personal bowel and bladder habits will inspire a pleasant transition to bathroom independence.

6. Inspire Peace at Mealtime

Telling the child what to eat and when to eat it takes away his power. You're headed for an emotional macaroni-and-cheese-on-the-curtains food fight if you don't approach the child with respect and kindness. For example, the children I presently teach eat lunch at school. They usually open their own lunch boxes. Invariably, a child will reach for the granola bar before the turkey sandwich. Before I intervene, I examine my own motives. Am I trying to control this 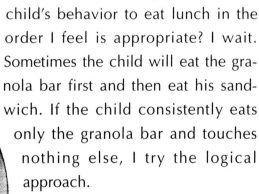 child's behavior to eat lunch in the order I feel is appropriate? I wait. Sometimes the child will eat the granola bar first and then eat his sandwich. If the child consistently eats only the granola bar and touches nothing else, I try the logical approach.

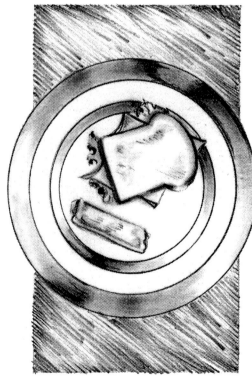

As soon as the child opens up his lunch box and reaches for the granola bar, I sit down, look into his eyes, and say, "I really care about you and what you eat." Then I point to the granola bar. (I do not take it.) "This has a lot of sugar in it. To get all your vitamins, please eat your sandwich first." Nine times out of ten, this approach works. I empower the child by allowing him to control the granola bar. Hopefully, I've convinced the child to eat the sandwich, too.

There are other issues to look at surrounding food consumption. I always talk to the parents to find out the child's total eating pattern. If the child eats sugary cereal and chocolate milk for breakfast followed by sugar-laden yogurt and graham crackers for lunch, then a serious sugar habit may be present. This issue needs to be addressed with the parents. Odds are this child is having concentration problems.

Don't make big deals out of things, or they will become and remain big deals. When I reason with a child (take the logical approach), I always whisper. This gesture in and of itself makes the issue smaller. Another way to attract the child's attention is to whisper, "I have a secret to tell you." Then whisper your concern in his ear.

Take time to consider your toddler's nutritional needs. Make sure the food he eats gives him an inner sense of balance and peace. The child's behavior always indicates when nutritional or emotional needs are not being met. Look into your own eyes, feelings, habits, and heart for simple, honest answers to your toddler's seemingly unexplainable behavior.

> *Look into your own eyes, feelings, habits, and heart for simple, honest answers to your toddler's seemingly unexplainable behavior.*

To ensure that the child eats a nutritious breakfast, you may need to get out of bed a half-hour earlier. The toddler will gladly "rise and shine" if you sit down and eat breakfast with him.

Demonstrate to the young child how to eat with a fork and spoon. As the child's hands strengthen, you can demonstrate cutting skills with a knife. Allow the child to feed himself even if half of it ends up on the floor.

Show the child how to clean up spills and remember that the toddler is perfecting a new skill. Nature didn't just graft wings together to make a butterfly. Allow the toddler to be a gooey, messy caterpillar for a while.

7. Allow Your Child to Develop an Intimate Relationship with Nature

I'll never forget the heaviness I felt in my heart on the first water day we had at our school (in Phoenix, Arizona, in 112-degree heat). The children, ages fifteen months to three years, brought their bathing suits to school. Mid-morning, we all went outside to partake in an array of exciting adventures: running in the grass under the sprinklers, sloshing through the mud, smearing our bodies with shaving cream, etc.

When we got outside, the children just stood there and stood there. No one moved. I couldn't believe my eyes. What a realization. My assistants and I had a calling to show these children how to have fun. So we traipsed through the sprinklers, sacked through the mud and covered ourselves with shaving cream. The children watched us and continued to stand there. Some of them even cried. Finally, a few of the children ventured out under the sprinklers and actually started playing and laughing. Others made it to the shaving cream tub. Some children were so traumatized that they had to go back inside. Two little boys cried uncontrollably because

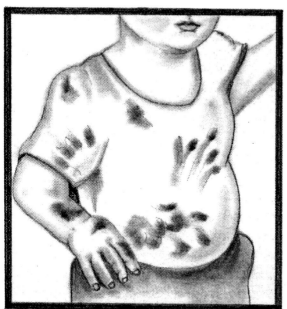

they got mud on their bodies. These children were afraid to have fun!

If we lived in the country by a stream or creek, our children would always be exploring and living in the many textures of nature. They'd be giggling while falling into a mud puddle. So would we. But in the city, our homes have white carpeting, our cars have leather interiors, and our furniture is bird's-eye maple. We insist on our children's cleanliness for the protection of our material things.

We spend hundreds of dollars on clothing for our children so they look good. The question is, how do they feel? Happy? Joyous? Spontaneous? Fulfilled? Are their needs for sensory exploration being met? Are they feeling one with nature and are their souls being fed? Wearing Guess jeans means nothing to the toddler.

Suggestion: Go to a second-hand store and buy special clothing for your family. Have designated "dirty" days. Allow yourself to sit in mud and dirt for a while.

8. Understand Your Child's Sense of Order

Every now and again, you'll find that the toddler gets hysterical over what you perceive as a small deal. For example, the child:

- needs to have the clothes hamper three inches from the chest of drawers

- needs to have the toy box closed at all times

- must have his favorite blanket available at all times, especially when you forgot to pack it for a vacation

- gets upset over three drops of water on a new shirt (Be careful of this one. If you are constantly changing, cleaning, and making sure the child is always perfect "no dirt, no water, no mucus, no food, no fun," you might be the genesis of the child's compulsiveness about cleanliness.)

The other day, I was on the telephone right outside of the classroom. The children were getting up from nap, putting on their shoes, and going home or out to play. I could hear a child screaming inside the classroom. My assistant came to me looking frazzled. She explained that Jack (two and a half years old) was in the midst of an emotional outburst. The assistant said that another child inadvertently put on Jack's shoes and wore them home. Jack wanted to go outside and all we had for him to put on his feet were his bedroom slippers. When the assistant handed him the slippers, Jack threw them across the room. That's what the screaming was all about. Jack wanted to put his shoes on, not his slippers. It's pretty hard for us to understand such a small deal.

Imagine you are going someplace very special. All of your friends are waiting to see you. Suddenly you realize that you're wearing pajamas and everyone else is dressed in formal attire. How would you feel?

Of course, we can laugh it off or go home. We have options. But to Jack, there is only one option: MY SHOES NOW! And that option is synonymous with his sense of order. What's familiar to Jack is his life and identity. Something as simple as having his shoes there when he gets up from nap is just as important to Jack as you or I finding our toothbrush in the bathroom after we get up in the morning.

> *It's up to us to provide the magic carpet that will immediately transport the toddler from the frightening and alarming world of change into the sanctuary of a safe new experience.*

Note: Because of your toddler's profound need for personal affiliation, it is important to remember that sharing isn't always okay. In fact, it can be detrimental. Make sure that your toddler has activities or toys that are distinctly his. Place them in a specific trunk or toy box. Have another toy box on hand that is designated for sharing.

Change is very difficult for the toddler. It's like falling off a cliff and not knowing there's a mountain of soft sand to safely land on. Children hold on to routines and habits tightly because it gives them a sense of security in this new experience called life.

A small change can really throw the child off-center. It's up to us to provide the magic carpet that will immediately transport the toddler from the frightening and alarming world of change into the sanctuary of a safe new experience.

Back to Jack. I went into the classroom to speak with him. I asked him if I could hold his hand. Holding Jack's hand while I looked into his eyes helped him to realize that what I was about to say was sincere. Looking into Jack's eyes, I said softly and slowly, "I understand your anger. Jonathan's wearing your shoes. I'm so sorry. We made the mistake. It's not your slippers' fault. Let's go get them." Jack picked up the slippers, put them on his feet, and went outside to play with his friends.

9. Replace Convenient Objects Used to Comfort Your Child

Have you ever stood in line at the grocery checkout stand in front of a wailing toddler stuffed tightly into a shopping cart seat? Then Mom takes a pacifier out of her purse and shoves it into the child's mouth.

What I see the caregiver communicating to the child is, "Here, let this object be emotionally available for you. Let the pacifier listen to you and comfort you. I don't have time."

In other words, the caregiver is ignoring the fact that the child developmentally needs to be walking and moving around. She is also overlooking the fact that the child has been confined in the cart for forty-five minutes, not to mention the number of times the child's need for sensorial exploration has been stifled (i.e., "Don't touch!").

The child quickly learns to transfer physical and emotional needs onto the pacifier. A pathological dependency is being created. Unavailability of that object as a way to "manage" feelings will surely instigate an emotional outburst.

Take a look at the potential consequences of using a pacifier to comfort your child:

- The pacifier might deform delicate structures that are forming in the young child's mouth.

- The child is not encouraged to use words to express his feelings. This can retard language development.

- The child becomes dependent on suppressing uncomfortable feelings with a quick fix (i.e., pacifier, bottle, etc.).

Could this be the genesis of a life-long pattern of addictive behavior? A young child stuffs a cookie into his mouth when feeling sad rather than going to Mom, Dad, or a trusted friend to verbally express that sadness and find comfort, support, reassurance, or a loving hug. What about the teenager who discovers that drugs, cigarettes, or stealing alters the ensuing depression that comes from denying feelings (i.e., anger, loneliness, sadness, fear, frustration, disappointment, shame, etc.)?

As caregivers of young children, how do we avoid inspiring this self-destructive behavior? We do it by modeling and encouraging verbal and emotional honesty. This begins with the infant. Talk about the emotions you see on the child's face. Affirm them. Talk about your feelings openly to the child. Let the child recognize that feelings are part of our humanness.

Observe your toddler for a day. Take notes of the emotional responses the child exhibits, i.e., tears, laughter, fear, anger (usually manifested as pushing, biting, hitting, etc.). Write down the event that caused the emotional response. Get to know the child's sensitivities. Honor and respect them. Sometimes a child just needs a soft touch or to be held. When it's time to rest, loving words, singing, peaceful music, or a gentle touch will lull the child to sleep.

My observation and experience is that the pacifier is a replacement for communication, reassurance, nurturing touch, and emotional expression. In other words, it's "junk love"! A rubber nipple secured to a plastic ring means nothing. Attached to a breast, a nipple becomes physical nourishment and tender loving care. If the mother cannot breast-feed for any reason, she can accomplish the same thing feeding the child with a bottle. This is not a replacement for the breast but an extension of it. It should be used only as the mother holds the child to her naked breast. This satisfies the child's physical and emotional needs in totality. Fathers are encouraged to hold and feed their infants in the same fashion, providing simultaneous sustenance, touch, and love to the child.

Mom and Dad intuitively will know when the child is ready to move into a very important plane of development—food independence. This is when the breast (or bottle) and dependence on Mom and Dad for nourishment are gradually replaced with the child's developing capabilities. Teeth are beginning to form, nature's way of signaling the infant's readiness to chew whole food. Muscular and skeletal structures are strengthening, enabling the child to sit at a child-sized table while holding and maneuvering a spoon or fork to feed himself.

At this stage, the child becomes aware that he is fulfilling two vital functions: sustaining his own life and caring for himself. These are the infant's first glimpses of independence, the foundation of his self-worth. Please refer to the chapter on weaning in Silvana Montanaro's book, *Understanding the Human Being.*

This means that once the child is weaned, all drinks are now served in a cup or glass. The continued use of a bottle, or replacing it with a pacifier, will confuse the child and promote painful emotional dependencies. To illustrate this point I'd like to share the following story.

Alex's Story

A two-year-old little boy named Alex enrolled in the toddler community several years ago. The first few days were challenging for him. He was never in a preschool situation before. Uncertain of the environment he was placed in, he held onto my leg as if it were a life preserver. I picked him up, held his hand, stayed with him constantly, even as I taught other students. By the end of the day, he was actually smiling but still physically and emotionally attached to me.

Toddlers need to feel loved and secure with the adults responsible for their care. Once these are established, the toddler will reach out to the enriched environment. A good attachment means a good detachment.

The next day, when Alex was dropped off at school, I accepted him into my arms as he cried upon separation from Dad. I continued to hold him. My intent was to show him that I was there for him and would not abandon him. When Alex stopped crying, I put him down. He walked with me around the classroom. After I gave a lesson to another child, I looked all around for Alex. He was sitting at a work table with an activity and was totally engrossed in it.

I observed Alex for a short time. After he got up from his work table, the newness of his surroundings *caused him to feel uncertain again. He began to cry. I immediately went over to him. I looked directly into his eyes and said, "I know you're feeling unsure. I'm your friend and I'm also your teacher. Come." I led Alex to an interesting and engaging activity on the shelf. I gave him a demonstration, then I walked away. He was fine the rest of the day. He had absorbed the fact that I was there to comfort him should he need me. At the same time, Alex was experiencing his own sense of security through the independent activities that gave him pleasure.*

The following day Alex came to school, he didn't cry when Dad said good-bye. Dad put Alex's backpack into his cubby and Alex walked right into the classroom and started working on a project. Midmorning, I noticed a child walk up to Alex. The child started interfering with Alex's concentration. In fact, he grabbed a picture out of Alex's hand, pinching Alex's fingers. Alex started to cry and ran over to his cubby, screaming now, frantically pulling his backpack out of his cubby. He tried to open it. His cries became louder and longer. An emotional outburst was taking place, exacerbated by Alex's frustration at not being able to open his backpack. I opened it for him. Alex threw everything out of it. He finally found what he was looking for: his pacifier.

I took Alex, the backpack, and the pacifier out of the classroom. This was very difficult to resolve. (Pacifiers are not an option once the child has integrated into the Montessori toddler community.) What a mixed message! If it was not an option, what was his pacifier doing in his backpack? Luckily, I was able to resolve the dilemma with lots of tender loving care and cartwheels (whatever works).

The backpack went back into his cubby, pacifier inside. But I observed Alex the rest of the day. He kept walking over to his cubby, trying to open his backpack and going out into the classroom again, choosing an activity, working until frustrated, going back to his cubby, crying, trying to get his pacifier. This happened continuously. I watched Alex, who was in the process of becoming self-assured, happy, concentrated, and independent, turn into an unhappy, easily distracted, insecure little boy. And all because he knew his pacifier was in his backpack.

I called his parents that evening and found out that this was the first day they had sent the pacifier with him. It was not in his backpack the first week of school. They sent it with him just in case he needed it. It's usually the parents who become dependent on using the pacifier. The pacifier in Alex's backpack became an inappropriate remnant of infancy that caused him to emotionally regress and distract him from self-actualizing into toddlerhood.

Special Note: It's okay for a child to form relationships with items such as stuffed animals, blankets, or sheets as a mode of self-comfort. These are transitional objects and not highly charged symbols of infancy and dependency. Thumb-sucking is also an appropriate way in which a child can self-nurture.

10. Communicate through Your Eyes

What would it feel like to be magically transported to a land where the language is foreign and everyone is two-and-a-half feet taller than you, where these people move at such a fast pace that it's virtually impossible for your little legs to catch up with anyone, let alone, your little eyes.

Courageously, you stay on your mission to make contact with one of these tall beings. It hasn't been easy. Just when you think someone is acknowledging you, it's hard to tell. There are no eyes to go with the bellowing voice.

Eventually, you start to feel invisible, like you don't exist at all. This creates an enormous amount of frustration and anxiety inside of you. The tension you feel revs up your metabolism and now your quest to make a friend becomes desperate.

Confused, your little body and eyes flit around from one stimulus to the next, trying to form some kind of attachment. But all you're accomplishing is an intimate connection to things. That just creates a deeper loneliness within you.

Finally, one of these tall beings bends down and looks into your eyes. Your whole body shakes in an attempt to flee. The habit of frantically moving and searching is so ingrained that it's very hard for you to stand still. But these two attentive, loving eyes won't let your eyes run away. Because they truly see you, and the healing begins.

Notes: _____

_____

_____

_____

_____

_____

_____

_____

_____

_____

_____

_____

_____

_____

3 Pausing to Look at Your Child

Developing a Teaching Relationship with Your Toddler

Maria Montessori understood the profound relationship between the teacher and the child. We are all teachers. As a Montessori toddler directress, a portion of my training was dedicated to the practice and demonstration of many exercises. These exercises were scientifically designed by Maria Montessori to meet the developmental needs and tendencies of the young child. (These needs and tendencies will be discussed at the end of this section.)

The prepared environment of the Montessori classroom includes autodidactic (self-teaching) materials in mathematics, language, practical life, sensory exploration, and culture. Practical life exercises teach the child basic living skills such as hand washing, vegetable preparation, metal polishing, etc. Sensory exploration exercises help to refine the child's sensory perception using smelling bottles, sound cylinders, tasting wafers, color tablets, etc. There are significant controls of error built into the materials to alert the child in case a mistake is being made. The directress (teacher) is still a profound liaison between the "work" activity and the child.

My responsibility to each child is to demonstrate the exercises in a way that will inspire the child's interest to repeat them. For example, I will invite the child to accompany me to the hand-washing table. I say, "Look at my hands. They're dirty. May I show you how I wash my hands?" Then I demonstrate handwashing to the child. I always include the child in the demonstration. I give the pitcher to the child and ask him to fill it with water. Then I pour the water in a basin.

Maria Montessori directed her teachers to pause and look at the child before points of interest throughout a demonstration.

Example: Place your hands into the basin. Lift your hands out of the basin and gently shake the droplets of water from your fingertips into the basin. Pause and look at the child. Take a bar of soap and slowly lather up your hands. After putting the soap down, leisurely massage your soapy fingers, hands, and wrists. Pause and look at the child.

Just recently, after several years of teaching, I realized the potency of these words. I finally understood Maria Montessori's keen insight into the student-teacher relationship and the importance of eye contact to nurture and strengthen that bond. Without a long psychological exposé on emotional bonding or the implications of its nonexistence, Maria Montessori just instructed me to "pause and look at the child." Just do it!

Clumsily, I struggled as a first-year teacher to entice a child to sit down with me for a lesson, let alone look into my eyes. As I tenaciously grabbed for teaching experience, I realized I could teach my students through fear (control) and consequence (time out), and they'd probably retain nothing—or **I could develop a teaching "relationship" with my students based on enthusiasm, joy, direction, attention, and respect, in which the child is excited to learn.** I now realize that a relationship includes honoring the child's being. This is lovingly accomplished through eye contact, even when there are no words. A fringe benefit of good eye contact is that you'll have the child's undivided attention. This will promote good concentration skills.

In the next section I will discuss children who have "tending" challenges. There are some specialists who call "tending" challenges ADD (attention deficit disorder). I prefer not to label young children as hyperactive or as having any kind of attention disor-

As caregivers, we need to find the source of the toddler's frustration instead of diagnosing the child's behavior as pathological.

der. I simply observe that the child is experiencing a type of anxiety or frustration. This frustration and anxiety is expressed through the child's body as excessive movement. Sometimes, this movement can disrupt the child's ability to "tend," or stay focused in the moment.

As caregivers, we need to find the source of the toddler's frustration instead of diagnosing the child's behavior as pathological. When Maria Montessori says, "Pause and look at the child," she says volumes to us. The phrase echoes the importance of a soul connection between teacher and student.

Healing and Preventing Attention and Speech Challenges

Attention Challenges

As a toddler directress I am very sensitive to habits that "young ones" create in order to survive. Unfortunately, these behaviors can interfere with the teacher-student relationship. My hope in working with very young children is that with parental support we can heal these behaviors and free the child to learn.

My first recommendation to the parents of a child with a "tending" challenge is **always look into the**

child's eyes during communication. When the toddler speaks, stop everything and attach yourself to the child's eyes. Say nothing. My second recommendation is **slow down your speech.** Exaggerate this response, at first, even if it takes three seconds to say one word.

These techniques work well to capture the toddler's attention. Sometimes, using these two techniques simultaneously will heal the child's "tending challenge." With some children, we need to dig deeper to find the source of the child's frustration and anxiety.

Some of these sources can include:

- Improper nutrition or food allergies—Check all labels and eliminate processed foods from the child's diet. This includes sugar and other carbohydrates, which might overstimulate the child.

- Not communicating with the child. This includes not listening, speaking for the child, not making eye contact during communication, delegating emotional bonding to nannies or siblings, and ignoring the child.

- Stifling the child's movement (i.e., placing him in a crib, walker, or playpen; carrying the child rather than slowing down and walking with him; strapping the child into a high chair, etc.).

- Stifling the child's need to mouth and touch objects (i.e., not providing child-proof environments).

- Constantly criticizing the child (i.e., expecting perfection and immediate obedience).

- Abandoning the child's physical and emotional needs once a baby brother or sister is brought into the home. This can also manifest in angry, hostile behavior that could threaten the new sibling.

- Not including the child in purposeful activities that contribute to the management and function of the household (i.e., helping to prepare dinner, sweeping, vacuuming, hammering, repairing, folding, sorting, etc.).

If the child has felt emotional or physical frustration for a long time, there is a physiological need for movement, which must be encouraged. Go to the park and run with the child. Walk swiftly in shopping malls. Allow the child to mop all of the floors in the house.

Another way to heal frustration, anger, or anxiety in the toddler is primal screaming. Shout to the mountain or the clouds, "I'm mad!" Think of all of the times the toddler felt life was unfair and just kept those feelings inside. I truly believe that the inability to express frustration and anger causes excessive movement in the young child. The good news is that it can be healed.

Jackie's Story

There was a little girl who was in my class two years ago. Jackie was thirty months old. This little girl could not stand or sit still for more than three seconds. In fact, every chance she could, Jackie darted out of the classroom. Once she was in the outdoor environment, she learned quickly how to unsecure the main gate. Jackie was telling us (in the only language she knew) that she panicked when feeling confined and desperately needed freedom. I immediately called her parents in for a conference.

After a long discussion it was disclosed that during the day when Jackie's mom was taking care of a younger sibling, Jackie was locked in her bedroom to control her behavior. Is it any wonder that Jackie became traumatized any time a door would close?

Along with good eye contact and slowing down all verbal communication, my immediate (intuitive) response was to create an environment for Jackie which afforded her "complete" freedom. Her parents cooperated fully. Believe me, it was not easy giving lessons to this child who was continually on the run. I walked briskly with her as I presented the primary colors.

Her parents no longer confined her into a high-chair at mealtime. They bought Jackie a child-sized table and chair and allowed her total freedom to come and go as she pleased. It took six months, but finally Jackie started to relax and her attention span increased daily. She was able to make eye contact and began making friends.

Unfortunately, stories like Jackie's don't always have a happy ending. David's story is one of disappointment and great tragedy.

David's Story
I'll never forget when David, his younger brother, and his parents first toured the toddler community. David was flitting around from room to room while I showed his family the school. He finally found the door to the outside environment and ran out. His parents stood there indifferently. I looked at David's

father. He was fidgeting and didn't make eye contact with me. I went outside.

I heard screams coming from a body pile-up on a little wagon. I ran over. David was sitting on Tyler, the little boy who had the wagon first. The child was pinned under David. David's parents were standing by the door, watching, taking no action. I held out my hand to David, looking intently into his eyes. I said, "I want you to get up."

David screamed at me, "No!" Tyler cried louder. I then gave David a choice. "You either get out of the wagon or I will help you to get out of the wagon." David shouted, "No!" He didn't budge. His parents hadn't budged, either.

I then reached down and put my arms around David's torso, trying to lift him off of Tyler and out of the wagon. David's body stiffened like a board, making it more difficult to maneuver him out of the wagon. I finally got him out. Then David proceeded to hit me. I backed away. David ran up to his parents. I could tell at that moment I was in for one of the greatest dramas of my teaching career.

David was now staring at me with hate in his eyes. "OK, let me show you the toddler classroom," I continued. We walked into my classroom and David immediately started to engage with the materials on the shelves. I introduced his parents to the various areas of the classroom and watched David out of the corner of my eye.

I observed a physical and emotional transformation taking place. The child who had been running around aimlessly was now sitting on the floor concentrating, disassembling and assembling the "Pink Tower." The Pink Tower is a series of ten cubes, each exactly one centimeter larger or smaller in size than the one before. They are designed to allow the child to sensorially experience the gradation of the cubes. David was building the tower perfectly.

David's face, which had been bursting with torment and red with anger, was now soft and pink. His eyes looked gentle. I walked over to him and sat down. I said nothing. I just observed him. When he was finished, he looked at me and smiled. I followed him to another activity, a fraction puzzle. I sat down on the floor to the right of him as he put the puzzle on the floor. I asked, "May I show you?" He looked at me, smiled, and said, "Yes."

I then demonstrated the activity to him. David attached his eyes to mine during the presentation. I could sense a trust developing. He knew I was there to respect and direct him. A deep affection and *appreciation emanated from his being. David started school a few days later.*

There were numerous instances of aggressive behavior instigated by him on the playground before class. David practically pulled Austin's arm out of its socket while trying to get Austin off of a swing. I looked at him intently and said, "David, I know this is your first day at school . . ." Then I held out my hand and asked, "May I . . . ?" He took my hand. Looking into his eyes, I continued, "We're gentle at school. May I show you gentle?" Then I very softly and lovingly touched his hand. "We also use words at school, not our bodies, to speak. Did you want a turn on the swing? Let's ask Austin." Then I modeled assertive use of language for David. "Austin," I asked, "May I have a turn on the swing?" By this time, David had run to the other side of the playground and was taking a shovel out of the hands of another child. I went over to him and modeled the same kind of behavior to him: respect, gentleness, and appropriate use of language instead of physical aggressiveness. Old habits die hard.

It was time to go into the classroom. David immediately went over to the Pink Tower and assembled and disassembled it at least five times. Then he found another task, which he integrated into his sequencing activity. I was amazed at the concentration skills of this three-year-old. He was totally self-absorbed and joyful in his repetitive attempts to perfect and expand his need for manipulation and exactness.

As another child stood by David to watch him work, David stood up and started to push him. I walked over. David looked at me and sat down again. The boy who had been watching David walked away. The time was perfect for me to introduce David to a "work rug." This is a piece of carpet that the child places on the floor and then puts his activities on. The carpet becomes a tangible and visual boundary reinforcement, not only for the wandering child who is looking for something to do, but also for the child who is using the carpet.

David loved his new sense of "boundaries" and the reassurance that his work was being honored and protected. I knew right away that there were probably problems of older siblings taking things from him at home, most likely in an aggressive manner. During my first consultation with the parents (that is, parent—only Mom showed up) my premonition was affirmed as truth. More was to be revealed, as well.

A few weeks later, David's dad came to pick him up from school. David threw a puzzle piece at another student as soon as he saw his dad. My next *conference with David's mother (his father had to work) was extremely insightful for me. David's dad had been on Ritalin ever since he was a child, and he never spent time with David. Though David had become very calm, concentrated, and loving with the children and staff at school, as soon as either one of his parents came to pick him up he became agitated and aggressive. I saw his dad grab David roughly by the arm one day. I could tell that David's parents were promoting his frustration and anger.*

David's concentration skills and self-esteem continued to grow daily, despite the discrepancies between his home and school environments. One afternoon I got a call from David's mother. She was crying hysterically. The family had just come from a psychologist and David was diagnosed as having an attention deficit disorder. It was recommended that he be put on medication. Tears welled in my eyes. I could not understand how any professional could make that assessment of a three-year-old who was not being observed in a familiar setting. Why didn't this psychologist come to David's school and observe him in the classroom before making any concrete decisions regarding his character? That diagnosis was absurd! David had incredible tenacity and concentration skills for a child his age. He had become a leader and example in the classroom. He continually gave presentations of the Pink Tower to the new students.

This was only the beginning of David's tragedy. Three months later, David graduated into the pre-primary classroom. The teachers in that classroom were not as overtly loving with David as he needed them to be. He began to regress and became quite agitated and aggressive at school. The next thing I knew, David was put on Ritalin and his behavior became explosive. One day, I heard ear-shattering screams coming from the pre-primary classroom. A teacher was trying to restrain David. This continued on a daily basis.

Finally, David was discharged from school. The last time I saw him, he had the glazed look of a wild animal in his eyes. I hardly recognized him.

My hope for all children is that their behavior be understood—not judged so quickly and medicated.

If it's behavior we don't understand, in all fairness to the child, we need to seek out interpreters who are capable of observing and understanding the toddler's language. The implication to "pause and look at the child" does not stop at the doors of the school or in a controlled environment designed to evaluate the child. It permeates every physical and emotional environment that touches the child's existence.

This includes relationships with siblings, parents, caregivers, teachers, etc. Young children are extremely vulnerable. Unhealthy relationships may lead to emotional and physical abuse, which can promote anxiety in the child. As caregivers we are responsible to the toddler to make sure everyone who relates to the child does so in a respectful, loving manner. Environments are also influential to the character and behavior of the toddler. It's imperative that the child's living environments contain the elements that will support his human needs and tendencies. Just like a washing machine comes to a halt during the spin cycle if the load is out of balance, you can expect the toddler's natural body rhythms to come to a halt if his basic needs for survival and growth are out of balance.

The implication to "pause and look at the child" does not stop at the doors of the school or in a controlled environment designed to evaluate the child.

Speech Challenges

Speech delays or challenges are similar in nature to attention challenges. Frustration or anxiety can cause a hesitancy for the child who is just beginning to say words, or for the child who suddenly feels insecure about talking. This insecurity can manifest itself in many ways. Stuttering is one of the most common. As with "tending challenges," it is most important to attach yourself to the struggling child's eyes when he is attempting to speak. Say nothing. In fact, speak to your child using silence. Your silence implies that you are finished talking and creating a clear runway for his self-expression.

Pay close attention to siblings who may be verbally striking down your toddler's words before they have a chance to get off of the ground. Always keep in mind that the toddler is just developing language skills and needs practice. Create as many scenarios as you can to reassure your toddler that what he has to say is important. Sit in a circle with the whole family and take turns talking or reading from a picture book. If you're reading a picture book, when it's your toddler's turn to share, wait to see if he'll look at a picture and speak. If not, you may have to subtly and gently—whispering—coax a few words from him. Point to a picture. Ask him what it is. Point to another picture, etc. Choose a picture book that you know will interest and excite your toddler.

It may take several sessions before your toddler trusts that his words can come out safely. If he's been cut off verbally for a long time, it may be very difficult for him to speak. Make a space for him, anyway—even when he says nothing. Do not speak for him or let anyone else try to fill in the void with their words. This is the toddler's time to speak, whether he's talking or not. Be patient.

Practice silence games by sitting quietly for a short time and then identifying the environmental sounds you hear. Play this game outside. Hear the wind blow through the trees, the birds chirping, and the whirling sound of the neighbor's lawn mower. It takes a lot of self-control not to talk, and can be quite uncomfortable at first. By identifying these sounds, you also will be enriching your toddler's vocabulary.

After awhile, the family's combined communication styles will balance out so that everyone will learn the pacing of talking and listening. Silence also befriends the individual who is unaware of his tendency to chatter over other people's words. A new world opens up for them. They learn that listening can be just as much fun as talking. Their relationships with others become richer and fuller.

Andy's story comes to mind.

Andy's Story
Andy started in my class at the age of seventeen months. His parents, Sarah and Jim, gloated over Andy as he explored the classroom. We spoke about his readiness to start school. There was no question in

our minds. Andy's wall-to-wall smile reflected his joy in finding a learning environment that was designed just for him.

He barely cried the first day of school because he felt so secure within himself. It was evident that his emotional needs were more than being met at home. "More than being met" was a good thing during Andrew's early toddler months, but as he started talking it became a handicap. His overly particular and expressive mother began dissecting his choice of words. Sometimes, she would cut him off mid-sentence. "Speak like a big boy," she would say. I never quite understood what she meant by that. I can't imagine how Andy could have, either. All Andy's mind and spirit could comprehend was that his message couldn't get through. Finally, this became a physical problem, and Andy started to stutter. Sarah called me at home one night, crying hysterically.

She was so upset that I could hardly understand a word that she was saying. She asked me what she should do. Should she take Andy to a speech therapist? Would he grow out of it? She shared with me about her uncle who had a terrible stuttering problem and how it has affected his life. I told her to take a deep breath. Then we proceeded to devise a joint plan that would provide Andy with a myriad of safe opportunities to heal.

Sarah made sure that she was always eye level to Andy when she listened to him. She also did a lot more listening than talking around Andy. Even when Andy got stuck for a second or two trying to get out the initial sound of a word, Sarah waited until he was finished to reply. The important point is that none of us reacted to Andy's stuttering. Sarah, Jim, and Andy played silence games and took turns communicating to each other, whether it be impromptu sharing or reading picture books. At school, my assistants and I did the same thing during classroom time with a small group of toddlers. Even the toddlers realized the importance of supporting Andy with silence. They didn't even notice his stuttering. Unfortunately, the stuttering became worse.

Sarah started to panic. She felt her son needed to go to a specialist. I supported her in doing what she thought was best, and at the same time the words of a dear mentor and colleague echoed through my mind. She had told me about the importance of not assessing or letting anyone else assess a child's behavior as being abnormal before the age of three. She also spoke of the imperative nature of consistency and familiarity in the child's healing process. In other words, whenever possible, make sure that the child has teachers he knows and trusts. Being around too many adults and being carted off to too many strange places can cause the child to become anxious. This might make matters worse. At this point, I prayed for direction. I still had a lot of faith in Andy to show us the way.

The next day I sat in the reading area of the classroom with Andy. We read a book together. When it was his turn to name a few marine animals, he got stuck on the "o" in octopus. I thought he would never get past it. The look on his face was one of terror. I was sitting to the right of him. I gently put my arm around his back and placed it lightly on his shoulder. The word came out clear as a bell! And so did the next word and the next word.

I was so excited that I called Sarah that evening to tell her of Andy's progress. I couldn't explain how or why the gentle touching seemed to free Andy from the tension that was holding back his words. There was only one thing I could be certain of: There are innate healing properties in observation, trust, love, and touch in all of us.

Sarah began trying this technique at home. So did Jim. The touch was very effective while working with Andy one-on-one. It was important that the sup-

portive touch be strategically timed, very subtle, and non-invasive. We only touched him once during each session, usually at the beginning when Andy was really stuck on a sound. Sometimes we waited several days before trying the touch technique again. Miraculously, Andy's stuttering slowly disappeared over time.

Toddlers are so resilient! That is why I love teaching them so much. Toddlers will tell us when something is wrong. In this case, Andy used his speech pattern to show us that he had a hesitancy to talk. All we needed to do was find the source of that hesitancy.

Learn to read your toddler before speech hesitancies become deeply ingrained. Remember that the "co" in communication means "together," "jointly," and "equally." I have included a Native American story called "Little Wind" in chapter 5 to illustrate this important point.

Designing a Home/School Environment That Supports Your Toddler

There is nothing difficult or overinvolved in setting up an environment within the home that will satisfy the needs and tendencies of the toddler. In fact, your home is a sanctuary in which the family unit is already functioning. Tasks and necessities for community survival and comfort are in place. Any room of the house in which the adult works, plays, or rests is an environment ready for the integration of the toddler. Little hearts are anxious to feel a sense of belonging and contribution. These feelings of worth can be instilled within the child in every room of the house. All it takes is a little creativity, observation and intuition (plus trial and error) to design space that the child might construct for himself.

It's 5:30 A.M. Our alarms go off. We find the off button on the clock radio. Then "somehow" we find the light switch to illuminate our way into the bathroom. . . . "Somehow" is through our dependence on the reliability of where to find the on-off switch on the clock radio. . . . "Somehow" is knowing that the light switch is within our reach and that we possess the muscular strength and coordination to operate it. So all of our "somehows" need to be the same "somehows" for the 3'3" little person to function in every room of the house.

Kitchen

Start with a night-light or a lamp on a table within the toddler's reach. Create shelving that contains the necessities for the toddler to function without the assistance of the adult. Make sure cabinets can be opened and closed by the child.

Bowls, eating utensils, cups, napkins, and food items can be easily managed by the two-year-old. Cereal can be stored in plastic containers, along with a scoop for serving. A bowl of fruit can be available to the child at all times. Have bananas ready with one starting slit to make it easy for the child to peel.

Make sure there is a drawer containing knives and other utensils specifically designed for the child's use. This includes child-sized cutting knives and spreading knives, a cutting board, spatula, whisk, and wooden spoon. Introduce a manual egg-beater once the child has sufficient coordination. Be careful not to set up the child for failure by introducing tasks that are not within his mastery. As always, use your intuition for "right" timing. Regular knives are good for cutting softer food items. Make sharper knives available for vegetable preparation (i.e., cutting carrots, cucumbers, etc.).

As the child learns to operate a sharper knife, accidents (cuts) are bound to occur. You can dull blades on knives and peelers (children love to peel carrots and potatoes) using an emery board.

Have plenty of oranges on hand for orange-squeezing. All you need is an old fashioned manual orange-juicer with a lip for pouring. The child will revel in making fresh orange juice for the family. Set up a child-sized kitchen table and chair for the toddler to eat all meals and snacks. Make sure it's adjoining the adults. Encourage the child to beautifully arrange his own eating space. This includes a tablecloth, cloth napkins, eating utensils, a pitcher for pouring, glass dishware, a vase of fresh-cut flowers, and wicker baskets for carrying all of these necessities.

Toddlers love to help prepare the meal. Design a work counter (adjacent to the adults) and delegate lettuce shredding, dough kneading, batter stirring, tomato cutting, potato mashing, toast buttering, fruit and vegetable washing, etc. to the child.

Make dishwashing a viable activity for the toddler. Create space using a step-stool for the toddler to reach the sink. You can also set up two basins, one with soapy water, one with rinse water, at the child's level. Secure the basins on a table, or have the carpenter of the house secure them in a wooden foundation. Don't forget to have a dish-drying rack of some sort to the right of the cleaning basins. Towels, child-sized sponges (cut a regular-sized sponge in half) and detergent (look for controlled bottles that require a shake or two for application) need to be in a cabinet or drawer that is toddler accessible.

Important note: Make or find a child-sized vinyl apron that is easily put on and taken off by the child. Velcro is an easy option. The apron signifies the importance and style of the task at hand. It is a gentle physical reminder that the toddler's work has begun, and once the apron is removed, the task is completed. Make an area available that houses child-sized mops, brooms, buckets, and scrub brushes.

Metal polishing is a useful and fun activity for the toddler. Place your tarnished silver on a tray with a nontoxic cleaner, cotton balls, and a cloth for shining. Leaf polishing is another activity that can be joyously executed by the young child. Cotton balls, a bowl of water, and a little oil can be used to clean and highlight the brilliance of houseplants.

Michael Olaf's "Essential Montessori" and "The Joyful Child" are catalogs that feature activities, apparel, and utensils that enrich the living area specifically for the child. Looking at the catalog will inspire creative ideas to make the kitchen a "home" and a purposeful place in which the toddler can co-exist and grow with the adult. (To order a catalog write to The Michael Olaf Montessori Shop, 1101 H Street, Arcata, California 95521, or call (707) 826-1577.)

Take the child out to the garden to cut a rose, and another, and another. Have a variety of vases on hand for flower arranging. Dried flowers work well, too.

"Children belong to nature."—Maria Montessori

Living Room

Create wall space that contains a mirror, wall hangings, and pictures that are eye-level to the child. Make sure the child can visually and tactiley explore everything in the room. Put fragile items in an enclosed cabinet so they can't be accidentally dropped and damaged while the toddler is perfecting fine motor skills during sensorial affiliation. Child-sized sofas and chairs can join the adult's furniture. Make sure the child has a table with a lamp, so he can control the lighting. Have a magazine rack available to the toddler with child-oriented magazines and books. A child-sized work table is perfect in the living room, where the child can sort and fold the laundry.

Remember that the toddler is in a "sensitive period" for movement. It is the child's work to design activities that lead to manipulation and independence. It is the adult's responsibility to provide a purposeful forum in which the child can satisfy the need to move and manipulate within the physical and emotional space of the family.

Forget the remote control, and demonstrate to the toddler how to manually operate the channel advance on the television set. Design shelving that is at the toddler's level. Place interesting modes of activity on the shelf for the child such as cards and objects for matching, puzzles, and transferring activities using objects that are manipulated by the pincer grasp (first three fingers) or tongs from one bowl or tray to another. Have fraction puzzles available to fulfill and inspire the toddler's mathematical mind.

If members of the household are reading in the living room area or listening to music that doesn't interest the toddler, form an entertainment center for the child with a cassette or CD player, a choice of his favorite tapes, and a set of headphones. Make sure this portable music player is lightweight and has a handle so the toddler has the choice of sitting or walking around while listening to the music.

The goal of the "living" room, as in any room of the house, is to have a variety of interesting and fulfilling activities that are geared to meet the "living" needs of the toddler, whether it be manipulating objects, enriching vocabulary, completing gradation puzzles, matching objects and pictures, listening to music, carrying trays, sorting laundry, dusting and shining the furniture, or serving a snack. The child will choose the perfect activity that will joyfully support his physical, mental, and spiritual growth.

Bathroom

The bathroom, as any other living area of the home, should provide all of the structural support and appliances that lead to the child's independence. The ideal situation in the bathroom would include a child-sized toilet, mirror, sink, and bathtub. This is not always practical, but a step-stool is.

Leave a special tray out on the counter with the child's toiletries. Include a toothbrush, toothpaste, child-sized soap dish with soap, hairbrush, hand lotion, and nail brush.

If possible, set up the child's area where it is close to the adults'. This way the adult will be a constant model of self-care and the child will learn by watching and then doing.

Hang bath and hand towels where the child can access them. Use solid warm colors that will attract the child. Loud colors or prints with cartoon characters will distract the child. As always, control the visual "noise" so the child can focus on the task at hand, such as brushing his teeth.

Bedroom

Place a lamp on a child-sized table inside the child's bedroom. The table can also function as a dressing table. Mount a mirror that is eye level to the child on the wall. Place child-sized combs and brushes in a beautiful wicker basket. The basket also makes these items transportable so the toddler can groom himself anywhere. You can put a little spray bottle of water on the table so the child can style his hair more easily.

Make sure the child has a chest of drawers that totally promotes his sense of responsibility. Drawers need to glide in and out easily. Rubber guards can be secured on each drawer to avoid pinching fingers. The young child can use a sturdy cardboard dresser. Avoid dressers overstuffed with too much clothing. Too many choices overstimulate the child. Three choices are enough. For example, in the sock drawer, place three pairs of socks with contrasting colors such as white, black, and yellow, or red, yellow, and blue. This will support the child in choosing socks that match.

Limit underwear, T-shirts, pants, etc. This makes the selection process, as well as the "putting away" process, easier for the toddler. On wash days, have a special laundry basket designated for the toddler. Delegate the child's choice of clothing for the week to the child. This includes carrying the laundry basket to the

laundry room, placing the laundry into the washing machine, adding the soap, loading the wet clothes into the dryer, folding the clothes, putting them back into the laundry basket, and putting the clothing into the child's dresser or hanging them in the closet. Make sure there is a rod in the child's closet that is the appropriate height.

Put shelving along the walls with baskets full of activities that the child enjoys. Place a few work rugs in a basket. Baskets are wonderful because they make the items portable and also help to organize the activities neatly and attractively. Keep the baskets earthen tones. Large toy boxes promote chaos and clutter. Too many items can be taken out at once, and the job of putting them back inside the toy box becomes too big for the child. Teach the child to work with one activity at a time and then return it to the shelf. Any toddler can handle the "putting away" of the items contained in one basket.

Limit the pieces placed in the baskets of the very young child. Increase the items as the child becomes more adept at sequencing. Avoid brightly colored plastic toys or overly stimulating decor in the bedroom or in any room of the house, for that matter. Keep colors soft and warm. Purchase collectibles for the children that are made from the earth. A toddler will gain a sense of oneness with nature by building with blocks made of various colors, weights, and textures of wood.

Shoe shining is an excellent activity to place on the shelf in a basket to enhance the child's sense of responsibility and for simple pleasure. Scuff up your toddler's shoe or find one that is already worn and scuffed. Place it in a basket with nontoxic scuff remover, cotton balls, a dauber, polish, a buffing brush, and a cloth for shining. When first introducing shoe shining to the toddler, limit the items in the basket. For example, start with a scuffed shoe, nontoxic scuff remover, and a cotton ball. Place a trash can nearby. Once the child masters these steps, add the polish, dauber, cloth, etc.

Outdoors
Make a work table available outside where the toddler can have access to child-sized gardening tools, rakes, brooms, etc. Provide shelving with various activities that the child can freely choose. Demonstrate flower cutting to the child and find a beautiful basket to lay the flowers in. Have plenty of paper towels on hand as well as a water source, so the towels can be dampened and used to protect the stems until they are placed in a vase.

A water table is an excellent water source for the child. You can find one in any children's outdoor activities store or catalog. Place funnels and cups inside the water basins to inspire water-transferring activities. You can also place sand in a tub or a basin. Each month you can rotate different objects into the sand for the child's tactile pleasure and language development. For example, you can place rocks and small logs on top of the sand and arrange an array of dinosaurs to make a scene.

Land-forms provide an interesting and engaging activity for the child. Find a medium-sized plastic basin or container and create islands, inlets, peninsulas, lakes, etc. using Styro-foam covered with green floral clay. Use blue floral clay to line the bottom of the basin, then build your simulated land. Make the land and sea arrange-

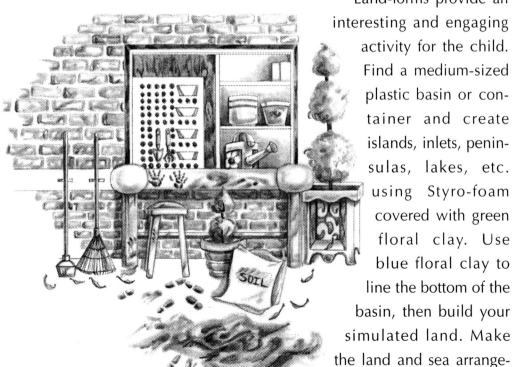

ment deep enough so the child can fill it with water. Create interesting tasks the child can do while learning the relationships in different natural environments. For example, place various ocean animals that float in the water and show the child how to fish for them, using a small fishing net you can find at any pet shop. Another idea would be to attach magnets to the fish and make a fishing rod that has a magnetized lure.

Other outdoor activities include wood sanding, using keys with locks (attach the key to a basket with a string so the key doesn't get lost), and furniture scrubbing using individual buckets, soap, child-sized scrubbers, and towels. Tires are also a tactile and visual wonder for the toddler to scrub. Make the toddler responsible for washing his own toys. Create a work area for building, sawing, sanding, hammering, etc. so the child can get a good physical workout. Make child-sized wooden planks for the toddler to hammer nails into. You can even draw a pattern on the wood so the child can hammer the nails to make a specific design. Rubberize the hammer head at first while the child is perfecting this new skill.

You can also pre-make a block of wood that has various-sized bolts attached. Demonstrate how to secure the nut onto the bolt for the child. As always, gauge the challenge of the exercise to the child's cognitive and physical readiness. For the child who is just beginning to gain tactile control and coordination, use one large nut and bolt. Once the child masters that one, present a smaller one, then one even smaller.

Toddler Needs and Tendencies

"Today the world is in a constant state of change. After a few years, new things will be old-fashioned. We know as educators that the principles of education are constantly changing."—Maria Montessori

The magic and agelessness of the Montessori method of education goes much deeper than preparing children for performance and profit.

"The society of man has not reached the standard of organization required by the advanced stage it has come to in the technical field. Therefore, what must be studied now are the needs of the present and not the organization of a better future. Although there's a wealth of material comforts, man himself has not kept pace in the making of individuals who can live better in harmony with humanity and nature. . . .

Man needs to live in harmony with himself."—Maria Montessori

This is Dr. Montessori's point of departure and motivation for identifying specific human needs and tendencies. The knowledge of these basic needs will help adults to prepare the child's environment so the child will construct his own human character, not mirror that of the adults.

Order

The young child is dependent on his surroundings because he is forming an important attachment and affiliation with this new experience called "life." Daily routines, textures, smells, sights, and sounds become new friends to the child who is grasping for understanding and reassurance that this new world is safe, precise, and reliable. A small change can disturb the child so deeply that he might become ill. Dr. Montessori says, "There's a place for everything and everything is in its place. Sensitivity for order in the environment is essential as breathing oxygen."

Orientation

Once the child feels secure and is at peace with these new surroundings, a yearning develops to understand his relationship to life. He begins to ask, "Where do I fit in? Am I male or female, White or

Asian, a big brother or a little sister?" Orientation is one of the first tendencies to appear in the child.

Exploration

Primitive man explored everything in his environment to find ways to satisfy his most basic needs, such as food, clothing, and shelter. Sensorial experiences for the young child (viewing, touching, and mouthing objects) are essential to promote a "knowingness" and freedom of movement. Child-proof homes and schools. Do not confine the child.

Communication

Children are drawn to words like bees to honey because they are innately sensitive to their mother tongue. Even though the words might not be totally understood, the child embodies the adult's loving intent to introduce a verbal bridge that symbolizes human feelings, thoughts, actions, and events.

Activity

Children automatically create scenarios where they can engage their bodies in some kind of physical movement. Watch the child in the kitchen, continuously washing dishes, never getting bored. Observe the child sweeping cracker crumbs from the floor or wiping a spill off of the table. The child seems tireless. Where does this need for continual movement come from? Maria Montessori tells us, "What we need to remember is that the child's actions are not due to random choice but directed by the child's inner need for development."

Manipulation

"I work with my hands and learn by doing. What I hear I forget, what I do I remember."—Maria Montessori. The child's energy of volition (willpower) directing his hands is essential to his mind's development. The action that occurs must be purposeful. Children know when activities are presented to them to relieve boredom only. The child needs things to manipulate that feed his sense of accomplishment and self-esteem.

Work

"I cooperate with others and with the forces of life. I use my hands to modify nature and make it work for my survival."—Maria Montessori. The hand reproduces the talent of man. The more intricate the work, the greater the attention and specification of man's intelligence. It is important that the child be given work to do daily that feeds his sense of community and contribution. We all have a job to do—policeman, butcher, crossing guard, etc. Let's not forget that the child needs one, too.

Abstraction

"Man's intelligent mind can create something that doesn't exist. He can use his imagination. Using his hands gives reality to what he imagines."—Maria Montessori. The Montessori method is based on introducing children to the real and concrete aspects of their new world before introducing abstractions. Examples:

- adding, subtracting, multiplying, and dividing quantities of rods and beads (units, tens bars, 100 square, 1000 cube) for tactile and visual comprehension before teaching the child their correlating numerical symbols

- looking at real things or pictures (i.e., animals, flowers, parts of a tree, etc.) and learning their names before introducing the child to their written descriptive words

- holding a solid wooden geometric sphere, rolling it slowly across a work rug, inviting the child to do the same, and then taking the child outside to identify other spheres in the environment, i.e., sun, orange, ball, etc.

Exactness

Precision fulfills man's need to serve the purpose of his mathematical mind. The child will innately begin to discern, investigate, contrast, and calculate differences and relationships in his new world. These are all manifestations of his mathematical mind. It is imperative to the toddler's development that he be given exercises to facilitate these tendencies. Create exercises such as pouring water from one pitcher to another, spooning rice from one bowl to another, or sequencing cards or objects on a rug. These exercises promote the child's aptitude of logic, judgment, reason, will to transfer, and exactness.

Repetition

Through repetition children learn to control and perfect. Why do young children repeatedly shovel sand into a bucket only to dump it out and start all over again? Why does a twenty-month-old take such delight in repeatedly taking off and putting on his shoes? There is an inner drive within the child to actively participate in skills that challenge him physically and psychologically. To inhibit that in a child would be like someone stifling our physical activity.

Wait before assisting the toddler in mastering any new skill such as buttoning pants, tying shoes, taking a jacket off and putting it on, carrying a heavy tray,

etc. Retrain your view of this situation. Close your eyes. Picture the child grunting and groaning at the gym while lifting a barbell. Growth can be painful. It hurts a little to watch.

Self-Perfection

Nothing equals the glorious feeling, or "explosion" as Maria Montessori calls it, of becoming a conscious master of your own body and spirit. Move over and let the child try to snap his pants for the fifth time. Finally, the snap is secured. Little eyes become intoxicated with joy. "I did it, I did it!" echoes from the lips of a little human being who is realizing his efficacy in a world of perpetual fumbles and mis-attempts.

Notes: _____

_____

_____

_____

_____

4 125 Activities to Awaken Your Toddler's Love of Learning

How to Give an Activity Presentation to Your Toddler

As a teacher, keep in mind that the greatest support you can give your toddler is an environment that will nurture his developing concentration skills.

Visual stimulation—Make sure there are not a lot of visual distractions on the walls, dogs running through the room, television sets going, etc. The goal is for the activity he is working on to have his *full* attention.

Auditory stimulation—Noise can definitely distract and interfere with your toddler's ability to stay focused. Shut off the radio and television and be aware of noises (or interruptions coming from other family members). When I am giving a presentation to a child and another child joins us using a loud voice, I immediately set a clear verbal boundary. I hold my finger up to my lips making a *shhhh* gesture and say, "I'm giving Susan a lesson. It's okay to watch." If you begin this technique early enough, you will save yourself a lot of headaches later on. It's amazing how quickly young children adjust to limits when they are always consistent. Eventually the child will internalize the limit and naturally respect his sibling's workspace and concentration. A side benefit is that the child who is watching learns, too!

Physical distractions—Don't let anyone interfere with your presentation or your child's activity. If another child or sibling tries to disturb or take his work, model the appropriate language. Say, "My work, friend," or "You may have it when I'm done." A work rug or table that is designated to each child helps to visually reinforce the physical boundaries you are teaching the children.

Now you're ready to give a presentation.

- Try the activity by yourself first. Make sure all of the items are available and operable to do the activity.

- Make sure the items used in the activity are not a choking hazard. Some toddlers are out of the mouthing stage and will be more interested in manipulating the items with their hands. If there is any question and your toddler puts everything into his mouth, use larger objects for the exercise and always monitor him.

- Think of the activity in terms of small steps. Demonstrate these steps in slow motion. This will insure that your toddler sees what you are doing. Let the child sit next to you, on your left side if you are right-handed, on your right side if you are left-handed. This way your toddler can see what the active hand is doing.

For example, feeding the dinosaur (number 8, page 133). Set the tray on the table in front of you, your toddler on your left (assuming you are right-handed). Make sure the bowl of beans is on the left-hand side of the tray and the dinosaur is standing to the right side of the bowl. Pick up the spoon. Pause and look at your toddler. Spoon up one bean from the bowl. While holding the spoon, pause and look at your toddler. Feed the bean into the dinosaur's mouth. (Make sure this is a dinosaur with a hollow inside to feed the beans into.) Repeat these steps until all of the beans are fed into the dinosaur. Use fewer beans for the toddler with a shorter concentration span. Increase the number of beans every few days. Once the beans are inside the dinosaur, turn the dinosaur over and pour the beans into the empty bowl. Say to your toddler, "Your turn."

Important Note: Use fewer steps for the child who is just beginning to concentrate. It will take a lot of effort for him to remember two or three small steps. The purpose of the presentation is for the child to watch (analyze) the steps involved in performing the task and then perform the activity himself. We are asking him to call on his newly forming comprehension skills. I have included variations in the activities that will advance the number of items and steps included to challenge your toddler's memory.

- **Do not speak when presenting an activity.** Your voice will distract the child from concentrating on what your hands are doing.

- **Make eye contact with your toddler in between steps.** This will help him to stay focused on what you're doing.

- **Have several activities set up so your toddler can choose the activity that he wants.** Make sure they are set up in such a way that there is enough room in between them so they are distinctly apart. Remember your toddler is just learning boundaries and it may be hard for him to discern one activity from another. Hand washing can be set up on its own little table. You can place two or three activities in baskets with ample room in between on a shelf. Make sure all of the activities are self contained and everything that is needed is in the basket or on the table. This way the child will learn to become independent and set up his own work area and begin the activity without you.

- **Set the activities up so your toddler works from the left side to the right side.** This develops his left-right eye swoop and strengthens his eye muscles for reading.

- **Never correct your toddler.** Walk away and let him do the exercise to the best of his ability. Present the activity again another time.

- **Help your toddler slow down and pay attention to detail.** Spoon or transfer one bean at a time. Squeeze the sponge until the last water droplet is in the dish. Clean up all spills on the mat with a sponge. Sweep up the last bit of rice on the mat with a small dustpan.

- **Help your toddler to complete the full cycle of activity.** Every activity will have a beginning and an end. During your presentation, include your toddler in getting the necessary materials (carrying the basket, getting the water, setting out the mat, etc.). Make sure your toddler also participates in all phases of clean-up. Soon he will be setting up and putting the activity away himself.

- **Make sure *most* of the baskets or trays can be carried by your toddler.** Show him how to use both hands when carrying a tray. I always have heavier trays and activities on hand that the toddler can aspire to carry with a little help from his personal trainer, me. I help the toddler carry these trays to his work area, challenging his muscular strength and coordination. Before I know it, the toddler is completely immersed in bodybuilding by carrying the tray himself.

Activities of Practical Life (Basic Living Skills)

1. **Cloth washing**
   Apron
   Cloths
   Pitcher
   Basin for washing

Basin for rinsing

Soap in a soap dish

Clothespins

Drying rack

2. **Doll washing**

Apron

Doll with clothing on

Basket for doll's clothing

Pitcher

Basin for washing

Washcloth

Soap in a soap dish

Shampoo

Large towel

3. **Dish washing**

Apron

Pitcher

Basin for washing

Basin for rinsing

Squeeze bottle of soap

Dirty dishes

Scrubber

Drainer

Dish towel

> **Activities of practical life help to develop your toddler's comprehension, ability to sequence, and independence.**

4. Hand washing

Apron

Pitcher

Basin for washing

Soap in a soap dish

Squeeze bottle of hand lotion

Hand towel

5. Nail polishing

Apron

Tray

Nail polish bottle filled with red-colored water

Emery board

Child-sized sponge for spills

6. Tooth brushing

Apron

Tray

A set of teeth (false teeth, play animal or dino-saur with teeth, etc.)

Small cup of water

Small tube of toothpaste

Toothbrush

Child-sized sponge for spills

Towel

7. **Dinosaur washing**

Apron

Tray

Dinosaur

Small cup of water

Soap on a soap dish

Brush

Child-sized sponge for spills

Towel

8. **Feeding the dinosaur**

Tray

Tall (10–12) dinosaur with an open mouth whose body is hollow inside

Small spoon

Small bowl of beans (fava, butter beans)

Variation—using the pincer grasp (first three fingers) to transfer the beans, feed realistic (play) bugs into the dinosaur's mouth.

9. **Shell brushing**

Apron

Tray

Large shell

Small cup of water

Small tube of toothpaste

Toothbrush

Child-sized sponge for spills

Towel

10. Mopping the floor

Apron

Child-sized mop

Bucket with soapy water

Dirty floor

Large towel

11. Table washing

Apron

Table

Bucket

Soap in a soap dish (can be applied in a small circular motion from the left side to the right side of the table)

Sponge for washing

Large towel

> *Showing your toddler how to wash and scrub using a circular motion prepares his hand and wrist for writing.*

12. Window washing
Apron
Window
Bucket of soapy water
Squeegee
Large towel

13. Bottle washing
Apron
Pitcher
Basin for washing
Assortment of small bottles with caps
Squeeze bottle of soap
Bottle brushes
Sponge

14. Water painting
Apron
Wall or sidewalk
Small bucket filled with water
Basket containing several paintbrushes (various
   sizes)

15. Water painting using sidewalk chalk
Apron
Sidewalk chalk

Wall or sidewalk to draw on using the sidewalk
chalk

Bucket filled with water

Basket containing several paintbrushes (various
sizes) for painting away the chalk drawings

16. Sponge squeezing

Mat

Dog dish (the left side filled with water)

Child-sized sponge for squeezing the water from
one side of the dish into the other (starting
from left to right)

> *Showing your toddler how to work
> from the left side to the right side
> strengthens his left-right eye swoop and is
> preparation for reading.*

17. Using a squeeze bottle

Mat

Squeeze bottle filled with colored water

Small sectioned dish to squeeze water into

Child-sized sponge to wipe up spills

> *Showing your toddler how to squeeze
> strengthens his hand and wrist muscles
> and is preparation for writing.*

18. Using a baster

Mat

Dog dish (the left side filled with water)

Baster for transferring water from one side of the
  dish to the other

Child-sized sponge for spills

Variation—eye dropper, 2 shot glasses

19. Using a whisk

Mat

Pitcher

Basin

Small squeeze bottle of soap

Whisk for making bubbles

Variation—food coloring

20. Pouring water

Tray

Pitchers with spouts or small glasses with lips

Colored water for variation

Child-sized sponge for spills

Variations—measuring cups, honey-bear jars
  with a funnel, vinegar carafes

21. Pouring beans

Tray

2 pitchers with spouts or 2 small glasses with lips

Beans, corn, salt, sugar, macaroni, etc.

Small dustpan and broom for clean-up

Variations—measuring cups, honey-bear jars, vinegar carafes, funnel

> **Showing your toddler how to pour, spoon, and transfer from left to right strengthens his left-right eye swoop and is preparation for reading.**

22. **Spooning**

    Mat

    Tray

    2 bowls

    Objects to spoon such as colored pasta, macaroni, corn, beads, rice, etc.

    Spoon

    Small dustpan and broom for clean-up

23. **Sweeping up**

    Child-sized dustpan and broom

    Beans or rice on the table

    Trash can

    Variations—child-sized floor broom, child-sized carpet sweeper

24. Object transferring using tongs

Tray

Tongs

2 bowls—one containing objects (nuts, beans colored pasta, buttons, etc.) for transferring one at a time into the empty bowl

Variation—fill one bowl with water and place floating objects in it to catch with the tongs and transfer

25. Object transferring using the pincer grasp (first three fingers)

Tray

2 bowls—one containing objects (nuts, beans, colored pasta, buttons, etc.) for transferring one at a time into the empty bowl

Variation—large wide-mouthed container, basket of potatoes

26. Indian corn tweezing

Tray

Large or small Indian corn

Flat square-edge tweezers

Bowl for corn kernels

Variation—2 bowls, one filled with colored beads for tweezing from one bowl to the other

> ***Showing your toddler how to tweeze and transfer objects strengthens his hand and pincer grasp, which prepares him for writing.***

27. Pumpkin scrubbing

Tray

Small pumpkin

Small water bowl

Soap in a soap dish

Small scrub brush

Child-sized sponge for spills

Towel

28. Blackboard scrubbing

Blackboard

Small basin

Scrub brush

Soap dish with soap

Hand towel

Variations—table scrubbing, tire scrubbing, toy scrubbing

> ***Showing your toddler how to scrub, polish, and shine using a circular motion prepares his hand and wrist for writing.***

29. Coin polishing

Ornate box with a few coins
Small dish of baby oil or nontoxic polish
Container of cotton swabs
Small vinyl mat for polishing coins
1/4 of a washcloth for buffing coins
Child-sized sponge for spills

30. Mirror polishing

Mirror
Small dish of baby oil or nontoxic mirror polish
Container of cotton balls
Small vinyl mat for polishing the mirror (can
   also mount a mirror on the wall)
Washcloth for shining the mirror
Child-sized sponge for spills

31. Silver polishing

Vinyl mat
Silver tray, pitcher, or other object
Container of cotton swabs
Nontoxic silver polish
Small polishing cloth
Child-sized sponge for spills

32. Leaf polishing

Mat

Small plant

Spray mister

Cotton balls or cotton swabs

Child-sized sponge for spills

33. Shoe shining

Mat

Child's shoe

Cup with petroleum jelly, nontoxic polish, or baby oil

Cloth for shining

Small cup

Dauber or toothbrush

34. Stringing

Thin ribbon, string, vinyl lace, or yarn (knotted on one end)

Pasta (colored), Cheerios or beads

> ***Showing your toddler how to string or sew improves his hand-eye coordination and develops his pincer grasp for writing.***

35. Sewing

Styrofoam, thick fabric, or square of oilcloth stretched onto an embroidery hoop (with small holes punched into the circumference for sewing)

Pincushion containing a thick, large, blunt needle pre-strung with embroidery thread (knotted on one end)

Scissors

36. Using a loom

Loom

Basket of weaving material to stretch over pegs

37. Rubber band stretching

Peg board

Basket of rubber bands

38. Clothes hanging

Child's-level clothesline

Basket of baby clothes or socks

Clothespins

39. Clothes folding and packing

Small suitcase

Basket of baby clothes

40. Napkin folding

Napkins stitched down the middle and on the diagonal so they are easy to fold.

41. Unrolling or rolling a rug

Small work rug

42. Sock rolling

Work rug or table

3 pairs of tube socks in a basket

43. Sock matching

Basket

Socks—red, yellow and blue, orange, green, and purple (start with primary colors first)

> *Showing your toddler how to match or sort trains his sense of sight and develops his discernment of colors, sizes, textures, and shapes.*

44. Sorting

Sorting tray or cupcake pan with individual compartments

Items to sort such as 2 buttons, 2 dice, 2 nuts, 2 shells, 2 thimbles, 2 coins, etc.

Variations—silverware into divider tray, canned
goods

45. Magnet matching

Mat

Bowl containing aquarium gravel in which 3
pairs of matching decorative magnets are
buried

Magnetic wand

Sectioned dish for matched pairs of magnets

46. Baby shoe matching

Basket containing different pairs of shoes, different styles or fastened differently (Velcro, buckle, tie, etc.)

47. Hair dressing

Mannequin head with hair (head should secure
to a small table or shelf)

Basket containing a comb, brush, barrettes, hair
clips, hair ties, hair combs, etc.

Basket of self-attaching rollers

48. Zippering, snapping, buttoning, or buckling

Embroidery hoop containing 2 pieces of material for zippering, snapping, buttoning, or
buckling

Small square frame with two pieces of fabric attached that zipper, snap, button, or buckle together

Parts of old clothing (purses) that zip, snap, button, or buckle together

49. Using a wallet

Wallet

Credit card

Wallet-sized photo

Currency

50. Opening and closing a lunchbox

Lunchbox (secured with a zipper or single latch)

Assortment of plastic containers

Napkin

51. Doll dressing

Infant-sized doll

Basket of clothes including diaper, gown, bib, hat, socks, etc.

52. Dressing up

Various hats on child's hat rack

Assortment of child-sized clothing and uniforms (military, nurse, fireman, etc.)

Chest of drawers containing jewelry, watches, etc.

Child's-level full-length mirror

> **Activities of practical life help to develop your toddler's organizational skills, self-reliance, and follow-through (full cycle of activity).**

53. Setting a table

Basket

Place mat

Dinner plate

Bread and butter plate

Glass

Knife, fork, and spoon

Napkin

Napkin ring

54. Crumbing a tray

Tray with a masking-taped square in the middle

Small dustpan and broom

Small bowl of rice, pasta or beans for dumping on the tray then brushing into the square before collecting into the dustpan with the broom

55. Flour measuring

Tray

2 bowls (one empty, one with flour)

Measuring spoon

Small knife for leveling flour in spoon while measuring

Small dustpan and broom for clean-up

Glitter (optional)

> ***Showing your toddler how to measure from the left bowl into the right bowl strengthens his left-right eye swoop and is preparation for reading.***

56. Salt shaking

Tray

Salt shaker with screw-on top (filled with salt)

Bowl to shake salt into

Funnel to channel salt from the bowl back into the shaker

Glitter (optional)

57. Salt packet tearing and pouring

Tray

Salt packets

Small bowl for salt pouring

Small bowl for empty packets

Variation—.75-gram salt packets are smaller and
require greater strength and coordination to
tear

> **Showing your toddler how to tear and
> peel develops his pincer grasp and is
> preparation for writing.**

58. Band-Aid peeling and sticking

Basket

Band-Aids

Smooth wooden board to attach the Band-Aids

Bowl for paper peeled off of the Band-Aids

59. Sticker peeling and transferring

Tray

Tape to make a line down the middle of the tray

Basket with an assortment of stickers to put on
one side of the tray to transfer to the other side

60. Eggshell crushing

Mortar and pestle

Wooden bowl

Supply of eggshells

61. Toothpick drop

Container of toothpicks

Sugar shaker with quartered spout

62. Opening and closing various objects

Mat

Basket

Bottles, jars, boxes, containers, etc. (with lids)

63. Using a spatula

Small cookie sheet or tray taped into 4 squares

4 sponges

Plate for transferring sponges onto

Spatula

> *Showing your toddler how to manipulate items whose equal parts make up a whole presents a sensorial impression of fractions and is preparation for mathematics.*

64. Using an eggbeater

Mat

Basin

Eggbeater

Small squeeze bottle of soap

Variation—food coloring

65. Play dough cutting, rolling or kneading

Mat

Container of play dough

Cookie cutters

Knife for cutting away excess dough

Variations—child-sized rolling pin, small shaker-bottle of glitter to knead into the dough, garlic press

Play dough recipe

1 cup flour

1/2 cup salt

2 teaspoons cream of tartar

1 tablespoon cooking oil

1 cup water

food coloring

Mix all of the above ingredients over a low flame on the stove. Stir until a ball is formed. Let the mixture cool. Divide into 4 parts, and using 2 drops of food coloring each, color the dough. Store in sealed bags or secure containers that will keep the dough soft and pliable.

66. Banana slicing

Basket of banana halves

Bowl for peel

Small cutting board

Knife

Sponge

67. Bread cutting

Basket of bread cut in halves

Small cutting board

Knife

Plate

Sponge

68. Apple slicing

Mat

Cutting board

Container of apple halves

Knife

Plate

Sponge

69. Carrot slicing

Mat

Cutting board

Container of carrots

Knife

Plate

Sponge

70. Carrot peeling or grating

Mat

Cutting board

Container of carrots

Peeler or grater

Bowl

Sponge

71. Orange juicing

Mat

Bowl of orange halves

Manual orange juicer with lip for pouring out
   juice

Cup

Bowl for rind, seeds, and pulp

72. Cutting

Basket

Strips of paper or pictures from a magazine

Scissors

Variation—cutting flowers in the garden

> *Showing your toddler how to cut and*
> *punch strengthens his finger and hand*
> *muscles and prepares him for writing.*

73. Using a hole puncher

Basket

Squares, circles, rectangles, or triangles made from construction paper or card stock

Hole puncher

> **Showing your toddler how to work with various shapes gives him a sensorial impression of geometry.**

74. Collage

Construction paper

Glue stick

Basket containing an assortment of objects to glue (cut paper, dried flowers, leaves, grass, etc.)

75. Festive easel collage

Easel

Sticky paper (contact paper) for lining the easel

An assortment of laminated symbols of Christmas—ribbons, tinsel, nativity scene, snowflakes, reindeer, etc.

Leaves for sticking onto the easel

Variations—all holidays; change of seasons; a variety of laminated leaves, flowers, etc.

76. Flower arranging

Basket

Fresh-cut flowers

An assortment of vases

Variations—dried flowers, artificial flowers

> **Activities of practical life help to develop your toddler's concentration, control of body (mind and body working together), and creativity.**

77. Mailing a letter

Tray

Stamps (self-adhesive)

Envelope

Basket containing an assortment of beautiful pre-cut paper to fit inside the envelope

Mailbox

Variation—child can color a picture for mailing

78. Rock painting

Mat

Rock

Watercolor paint set

Paintbrush

Small cup of water

Sponge for spills

79. Rubber stamping
Mat
Construction paper
Assortment of rubber stamps
Ink pad
Variation—different colored ink pads

80. Candles and candle holders
Mat
Single or double candle holder
Basket
Assortment of candles
Variations—candelabrum, menorah

81. Pencils and erasers
Tray
Small basket with pencil halves
Small basket with erasers to fit the pencil ends
Pencil holder for finished product
Variation—colored pencils with erasers that
match

82. Pencil sharpening
Tray
Pencil holder
Pencils
Pencil sharpener

83. Locks and keys

Tray

Basket holding 2 small locks

Basket holding 2 small keys

> **Showing your toddler how to manipulate items whose pieces fit together improves his hand-eye coordination and develops his pincer grasp for writing.**

84. Nuts and bolts

Tray

Basket containing 2 different-sized nuts and bolts

85. Using a hammer

Small hammer

Soft board

Container

Nails with large heads

Variations—tree stump, table

86. Assembling and disassembling a flashlight

Mat

Basket

Flashlight (without springs)

Batteries

Activities to Refine the Senses

87. Sound bottles

2 bottles, 1 containing a small quantity of beads that make a loud sound when shaken, 1 containing a quantity of smaller beads that make a soft sound when shaken

88. Musical glasses

Tray

3 or more glasses, each filled with water

Mallet for striking

Variation—colored water

> *Activities that demonstrate sound help your toddler to develop his listening skills, memory, and concentration.*

89. Sound games

Homemade cassette tape containing sounds from the environment such as dog barking, faucet dripping, vacuum cleaning, corn popping, baby crying, etc. (made with ample space between each sound)

"Sounds of the World" tape found in teaching materials stores containing sounds such as marching bands, violins, herds of sheep, trains, bagpipes, etc.

Variation—blindfold

90. Smelling bottles

Mat

3 tightly secured shaker bottles, each containing a cottonball drenched in a particular essence, such as perfume, garlic, peppermint oil, cloves, etc.

> ***Activities that demonstrate the sense of smell and taste help your toddler to become aware of the relationship between these two senses.***

91. Tasting wafers

Chinese edible rice paper cut into bite-size pieces, placed on a plate

3 little jars filled with various substances that taste distinctly different such as salt water, sugar water, bitters, lemon juice, etc.

Droppers to place small amount of substances onto rice paper for tasting

92. Sensorial extravaganza

Sturdy, large barrel, tub or wading pool (that your toddler can comfortably sit in)

Several large bags of beans, rice, peas, or a combination

93. Rough and smooth boards

A board divided into 2 squares, one covered with rough sandpaper, the other smooth polished wood

Variations—soft and hard, wet and dry

> ***Activities that demonstrate different textures, weights, and temperatures help your toddler to develop keen skills of discernment and comparison.***

94. Touch tablets

Box containing several tablets covered with different materials such as felt, leather, vinyl, Velcro, etc.

Blindfold (optional)

95. Fabric box

Box containing definite contrasting fabrics such as silk, linen, wool, fake fur, denim, tweed, leather, etc.

Blindfold (optional)

96. Fashion beanbag and quilt matching

Basket

An assortment of square beanbags (polka dot, stripe, plaid, herringbone, paisley, tweed)

Quilt made with corresponding squares of fabric (make sure there are ample borders of a solid neutral fabric in between the squares)

97. Weighing wooden tablets

4 tablets—2 made from light-colored, lightweight pine, 2 made from dark-colored, heavyweight walnut. Tablets must fit in the palm of the child's hand for weight comparison

Blindfold (optional)

98. Hot and cold bottles

2 small tightly secured bottles—one containing hot water, the other containing cold water

Variations—ice pack, heating pad, heater, air conditioner

99. Making a rainbow

Prism

Windowsill

Sunlight

100. Mystery bag

Beautiful bag secured by a drawstring

Assortment of things inside with various distinct
textures—pine cone, feather, crystal, modeling
clay, velvet cloth, etc.

Blindfold (optional)

> *Covering your toddler's eyes with
> a blindfold will heighten all of his
> other senses, forming a visual image
> of an object.*

101. "Big and little" matching

Large basket containing items that are the same
but one is little and one is big—1 small screwdriver and 1 big screwdriver, 1 small apple
and 1 big apple, 1 small bear and 1 big bear,
etc.

2 smaller baskets—one for little items, one for
big items

Variations—thick and thin, tall and short, wide
and narrow

Blindfold (optional)

102. Primary color matching

Felt mat

Basket

6 spools of thread—2 red, 2 yellow, 2 blue

Variations—tablets, tiles

Activities for Language Development

103. City walk

Take the child into the city—show him a bus, taxi cab, street light, jewelry store, sandwich shop, old house, burnt house, workman working on a roof, colored lights (Christmas is coming), pumpkins in windows (Halloween is coming), spicy smells from the bakery (Thanksgiving is coming). Give him the words that go with the action of life surrounding him.

104. Nature walk

Take the child out in nature—show him new leaves on a tree (spring), a tree growing flowers (summer), leaves on the ground (fall), snow (winter), a hill, a lake, a rock, a boulder, a river, sand, etc. Give him the words that describe the beauty surrounding him.

105. Nature basket

Felt mat

Basket containing real items found in nature—leaf, acorn, flower, pod, pinecone, pussy willow, etc.—to display on the mat (3 at a time; increased to the child's growing attention span)

106. Fruit basket

Felt mat

Basket containing an array of fresh fruit (if not available, use real-looking simulated fruit) to display on the mat (3 at a time; increase to the child's growing attention span)

Variation—vegetable basket

107. Animal basket

Felt mat

Basket containing an assortment of animals (farm, wild, rain forest, etc.) to display on the mat

Variation—animals and their young (pig, piglet; horse, foal; cow, calf; etc.)

108. Identifying household items

Work rug

Bag containing real items found in the home—
shoehorn, watch, perfume, can opener, tape
measure, etc.—to display on the work rug.
Begin with 3 objects, increase to 6, etc.

Variation—categorize items found in each room,
(kitchen, bathroom, etc.)

> ***Showing your toddler new objects will
> increase his vocabulary and help him to
> classify and perceive order within his
> environment.***

109. Object presentation for enrichment of vocabulary

Felt mat

Object basket or mystery bag containing real-
looking objects—car, cat, book, violin, shoe,
etc. to display on the mat. Begin with 3
objects, increase to 6, etc.

110. Categorical object arranging using clay

Basket or bowl

Floral clay

Props for scenery—rocks, wood, grass, street
signs, etc.

Objects—bugs, dinosaurs, cars, trees, etc.

Begin with 3 objects, increase to 6, etc.

Variation—farm scene with barn, animals, and fences

111. Beginning phonetic sound categorical objects

Felt mat

A small organizer box with 26 pull-out drawers (found in a hardware store)

26 labels—A to Z—to place individually on the front of each drawer

Assortment of objects that begin with corresponding beginning phonetic sounds to go into each drawer (refer to page 5)

Present 1 consonant or 1 vowel drawer at a time (adjust to toddler's growing attention span)

112. Beginning phonetic sound categorical objects or pictures

Felt mat

26 small boxes, labeled A to Z

Assortment of objects or pictures that begin with corresponding beginning phonetic sounds to go into each box (present 1 box at a time)

Once the child becomes familiar with the objects and pictures, replace them with new ones to challenge him

113. Object-to-object matching

Work rug

Basket

6 objects—3 sets of same object for matching (Increase the number of objects to the toddler's growing attention span)

Variation—match objects that are similar (of the same category but not exactly alike)

114. Object-to-picture matching

Work rug

Basket

3 pictures

3 objects that match the pictures (Increase the number of pictures and objects to the toddler's growing attention span)

Variation—match objects to pictures that are similar but not exactly the same

115. Object-to-silhouette matching

Work rug

Basket

3 related objects such as tools—hammer, wrench, screwdriver

3 pictures that are an outline drawing that matches each object

Variations—leaves, dinosaurs, etc.

> ***Showing your toddler how to match objects to their corresponding silhouettes helps him to refine his discrimination of shape and form.***

116. Picture-to-picture matching

Work rug

Basket

3 sets of same pictures for matching (increase the number of pictures to the toddler's expanding concentration skills)

Variation—matching pictures that are similar but not exactly alike

117. Split picture matching

Work rug

Basket

3 pictures of simple individual objects cut in half

118. Sequential picture matching

Work rug

Basket

Sequential pictures—spring, summer, fall; soil, seed, plant; letter, mailbox, mailman

Begin with 3 pictures, expand number of pictures to the toddler's increasing attention span (usually expand the number of pictures in increments of 3)

119. Presentation of individual pictures for enrichment of vocabulary

Work rug

Basket

Pictures (begin with 6) that depict different aspects of our culture—geography (land, water, mountain ranges, waterfalls, seasons, climate etc.), biology (parts of the body, land and sea animals, fish, birds, etc.), botany (leaves, flowers, trees, etc.), astronomy (day and night, sun, moon, etc.)

120. I spy (objects)

Felt mat

Basket

6 objects to display on the mat for the child to recognize; "I spy a rhinoceros. Place it in my hand," "I spy a carousel. Place it on my knee," etc.

121. I spy (beginning sounds)

Felt mat

Basket

3 objects to display on the mat whose beginning sounds your toddler can recognize; "I spy something that begins with an 'm'"

122. Shape tracing

Simple geometric puzzle with knobs for holding onto the pieces—circle, square, triangle, rectangle

Plain white paper

Pencil holder

Child-sized pencil for tracing the puzzle shapes onto the paper

Variation—simple-shaped puzzles such as dinosaurs, tools, food items, etc.

> *Showing your toddler how to hold and direct a pencil while tracing a puzzle piece develops his muscle control for writing.*

123. Colored pencil matching and shape tracing

Simple, geometric-shaped puzzle with knobs containing different-colored shapes—red, blue, yellow

Plain white paper

Pencil holder

Child-sized red, yellow, and blue pencils to trace around corresponding colored shapes

Variation—superimpose different colored shapes on top of one another

Activities to Introduce Mathematics

124. Fruit cutting

Mat

Knife

Orange for cutting in half and then quarters

Cutting board

Bowl

Variation—apples, pie, cake; draw circles, squares, rectangles, and triangles and cut

> *Showing your toddler how to cut items whose equal parts make up the whole presents a sensorial impression of fractions and is preparation for mathematics.*

125. Object counting

Felt mat

Basket

3 objects that are identical—nuts, buttons, grapes, etc.

Once the toddler knows 3, increase number of objects by increments of 1; stop at 10

> *Showing your toddler how to count to ten using identical objects helps him to understand the relationship between the exact quantity and the name of its corresponding number.*

5 An Illustration of the Importance of Language and Communication

A Final Thought

The art of communication never stifles. It creates time and space that nurtures understanding between people. To illustrate this important point I have included my story of Little Wind. It is a reflection of my life experience through the eyes of a Native American child.

My best to you and your children...

Little Wind

A-ho, friend. I am Little Wind, daughter of Speaks Many Words and Breeze of Cool Water. As a small child, I had a different name.

Mother, Breeze of Cool Water, would rock me in her arms. Calm and peaceful, I would drift off to sleep. Then she would tie my blanket like a hammock to the inside of the tepee and go outside to gather chokecherries and plums for us to eat.

One day, I woke up before Mother came back. I waited and waited for the buffalo hide walls of the tent to shake and the smell of sweet fruit to tell me she was home.

When she didn't come for a long time, I started to cry. Then, I heard a songbird. Happiness filled my heart.

I opened my mouth and from my lips many beautiful sounds danced into the air. Before I knew it, Mother was standing over me, listening to my song and smiling.

Father, Speaks Many Words, was far away and heard the enchanting melody. He followed its call, riding his painted pony across the plains.

There was a sparkle in his eyes when he saw the magical sounds came from me—the tiny one with no name, who could not yet speak. "My child," he said, "The Great Spirit has placed within you your name. You are Songbird."

Other tribes learned of my gift and traveled from far away, crossing mountains to hear me sing. They brought elk hide–covered bowls filled with pebbles that made music and tiny beaded dolls for me to play with.

Long winters passed, and Mother began teaching me the ways of a young girl. As we worked together, I watched Mother's mouth. Her words always matched what was in her hands and heart. Pretty soon, I could speak words, too.

Each night, Father came home from hunting, looked around the lodge and asked me what I had learned. Happy to use my words, I answered, "Today, Mother showed me how to grind corn, cut elk, make beau—" "Make beautiful fringe," interrupted Father, "What else did you learn?"

Anxious to use my words again, I answered, "Today, Mother showed me how to—" "Say no more, little one," said Father. "I must go and speak to Fast Eagle about the ponies now."

I ran out of the tepee and found a quiet place along the river to sit. A tear made ripples through my reflection in the clear water. Father returned and handed me a deerskin dress, a gift from Fast Eagle. He asked me what I saw in the water.

"Father, in my eyes I see such sa—" Before I could tell him of my sadness, he said, "It is clear, Songbird, you only see your reflection and not the beauty of this dress I have brought for you."

Many snows came and went. Father would listen with others to my songs but never let me finish my spoken sentences.

It was time for my childhood name to be changed. Father called the medicine man into our lodge. For the ceremony, the medicine man asked me the season of my birth. Instead of saying, "After the cold has turned the leaves red," I said, "After the cold ha—"

The words stopped coming.

"Speak, Songbird," said Father.

I tried again. "After the co—," but the rest wouldn't come out. "Then sing, Songbird," pleaded Father.

"Ah, ah," I stammered. There was no music.

"The Great Spirit has placed within you a new name," Father said with a heavy heart. "Since there is no breath to finish what you speak or sing, you are Little Wind."

Lightning bolts cracked open the sky and thunder pounded the heavens. The medicine man laid me down on a soft bed of eagle feathers. He put wet roots, grass, and leaves on my throat. "When Little Wind is strong," said the medicine man, "she will speak her truth."

Father followed the medicine man quietly outside of the tepee. I fell asleep.

When I awoke, I sang my dream. Chipmunk, Rabbit and other forest children stopped by to listen. Father heard my song and came inside the tepee. I tried to speak. Nothing came out but soft sounds.

"Debwewin (Oh, Great Truth)," I whispered, "please give me the words to tell Father."

Truth Spirit answered my prayer.

"Father," I said, "when I was Songbird, my sounds like tiny babies were cradled in silence and grew for all to hear. But as I started to speak words, you spoke whenever you wanted even if it was in the middle of what I was saying. It was Speaks Many Words, not the Great Spirit, who scared my breath away and made me Little Wind."

Father took my hand. I saw tears in his eyes. "Come," he said. "Let's walk."

Our words fell to Earth like falling leaves, one by one, in harmony. They filled her with love and wisdom until the stars flickered in the night sky.

Father wanted to change my name back to Songbird, but the medicine man said, "If we look only to her as Songbird, we may forget that Little Wind had much to say. Her name shall remain as a message and reminder to all people. A-ho, friend."

THE END

ABOUT THE AUTHOR

Jan Katzen-Luchenta is the director of a cozy Montessori toddler house located in the historic district of downtown Phoenix, Arizona. She lives in Phoenix with her husband, Joe. Jan spends her free time composing music on the piano, writing children's stories, and presenting color box one (the primary colors) to her African Grey Parrot.

To contact the author for a personal consultation, workshop information or to share your ideas and experiences, write to her at:

Emunah Publishing Company
PO Box 45148
Phoenix, Arizona 85064

or e-mail her at: TodlrTcher@mindspring.com

ABOUT THE ILLUSTRATOR

Carrie Follrad-Klein is a freelance illustrator and dedicated mother. She lives in Mesa, Arizona with her husband, daughter, sister and brother. Carrie has illustrated several fairy tales and enjoys drawing children's portraits. Carrie would like to dedicate her illustrations to her daughter, Tabitha and husband, John.

To order additional copies of *Awakening Your Toddler's Love of Learning*, send a check or money order for $15.95 plus $3.50 shipping and handling to:

Emunah Publishing Company

PO Box 45148

Phoenix, Arizona 85064

(If ordering more than one book, add $.50 per book to the $3.50 shipping charge.)